Live Free or Die

Reclaim your Life... Reclaim your Country!

SHONA BANDA

authorHOUSE®

AuthorHouse™
1663 Liberty Drive
Bloomington, IN 47403
www.authorhouse.com
Phone: 1-800-839-8640

© *2010 Shona Banda. All rights reserved.*

No part of this book may be reproduced, stored in a retrieval system, or transmitted by any means without the written permission of the author.

First published by AuthorHouse   5/28/2010

ISBN: 978-1-4490-4557-9 (e)
ISBN: 978-1-4490-4555-5 (sc)
ISBN: 978-1-4490-4556-2 (hc)

Library of Congress Control Number: 2010907861

Printed in the United States of America
Bloomington, Indiana

This book is printed on acid-free paper.

A note to the reader...

As you begin this journey I must remind you now that I am very alive and very well. What you are about to read will be very hard to read... but read you must, to be able to understand what a miraculous recovery I have now accomplished. I attest now that this book started as a journal to record my progress on an experiment of medication for my body. The results were so spectacular that I knew it was instrumental to put it all down on paper.

I am in what I now believe to be a deep-seeded remission from a debilitating disease. I am and will always be *healthy, vibrant, awake, aware, and alive* as long as I have my medication. I am hopeful that this may be a cure to many things, however **I am not legally qualified to make that determination.** I do *know* that you will be able to make your own decision once you have finished this journey...

As you are about to embark on an adventure of your very own!

CHAPTER 1

PHILOSOPHY?

I had never understood the actual concept of philosophy ...until now, at least in my mind, I think. It is nothing more than opinion, a kind of science and mythology combined to find real answers, only to find more questions, leading you to always thirst for knowledge, always feeling as if you never know enough. Theories and guesses on everyday life and the how and why things work. One must look at philosophy just as seriously as he or she would look at anything else.

I feel that a proper education is not actually bought or paid for, or found at any "community college." It is the proper education of a person to find truth and knowledge on their own. Self motivated self-searching, for truth and answers. Looking at all angles of any information given—whether on TV, the Internet, or in a textbook. Looking at them as they really are ... someone else's interpretation of knowledge. Yes an opinion. **Everything is opinion**. When you sit back and look at the world, you will realize a very simple little thing—another person's opinions have paved the way for everything .... Wow! That is a lot to take in.

Now think of what personal liberty really means. It means that your opinion counts too. One must be curious and intrigued by any information that comes in front of them. If the slightest intrigue is missing, you will not care and therefore not learn said information. Only the strong and persistent will survive in this strange, unyielding world that we have recently inherited from our ancestors.

Self-taught knowledge is the one and only thing that will help us all survive as a species. Relying on our current political system for education at this point seems redundant. Seeing the implications on a mass scale brings thick politics in the mix and that, in our day and age, brings only corruption.

When I was a child, I had to know the "basics" before I was allowed into the school system at the age of five. That put the responsibility on my mother to take the time to teach me my basic shapes, colors, ABCs, and 123s. Now with my second child finishing up his first year of preschool—of course I had taught him his basics before he started—I have realized something dire. The public school system spends the entire year of preschool only learning the basics. The system has made it easy for parents to become lazy and to no longer work with their children. The government will teach your children all they need to know (without college, of course).

The "dumbing down" of America is a very real thing! I am a perfect example! My education in the public school system consisted of sitting in a small classroom with forty to fifty kids for one teacher to try to calm down and teach. There was absolutely no time for one-on-one attention. As an adult, yearning for more knowledge—and, more importantly, finding the knowledge and retrieving what was needed from it—has formed the person I am today. I know my children will be able to understand and retain the real knowledge out there. Reading many books, the gears in each of their brains will grind and click away with light bulbs of ideas forming left and right.

Our family is meant to do great things! I can feel it at the core of my soul. Teaching my children now, excellent values, high moral standards, and leadership skills; I hope to make their journey through life filled with the kind of success you can look at filled with so much pride that you feel as if it might explode. I teach them to always take pride—and the time—to do things the right way the first time; To think things through, to always look at a problem from all sides, and to put themselves in situations (theoretically) of others to help them solve any problem that may arise.

The point is ...that the knowledge is out there, the Internet is a wonderful tool! If used properly, information can be easily achieved. It is also up to me as a parent to make sure that my children are just as—if not moreso—educated than both of their parents combined by the time they are ready to leave the nest. I have made a conscious effort to look outside the box as well as within. I hope to pass that on to my children who I know are meant to be great leaders one day—leaders and controllers of their own lives and liberties, leaders of their families, and moral mentoring leaders to their friends. Great leaders, which will always do things in a just, and fair way.

In that way, they will be **Great Leaders, Great Thinkers,** and **Great Movers** in anything they try to accomplish.

Realizing the realization of all knowledge will always lead anyone down the rabbit hole of truth!

3-30-09

CHAPTER 2

The Beginning ...

I have come to the conclusion that I must write about my past in order for those who may not know me personally to understand all my body has been through. My friends, my family, and even my physicians over the years do not realize the extent of damage. Pride has always come to the table whenever I had described any part of my sickness to anyone other than my husband—even from my children. When mommy was not feeling well, she was in the garage. I kept myself away from them because I never wanted them to see me grimace in pain or cry out. So I kept a bit of a distance. In some ways, I regret the time away from them; and in some ways ... I don't. No child should have to watch their mother in pain like that. I now have that miraculous second chance at life! I am going to take full advantage! My children will know who I am before I am gone, which had been a major issue with me. I had come to the conclusion that I would pass at a very young age, and that my children would only remember their sick and lifeless mom ... very depressing. For the first time, I am able to envision a great future and living a long and healthy life. I might even get to meet my grandchildren someday, whereas to before, I was not even able to imagine or picture staying on this earth long enough.

My husband is my backbone. I could not have asked for a better man to have been the father of my children or to have stuck through and been by my side every step of the way. Our love over the years truly has deepened more and more as time goes by. Now, at fairly young ages, we are forced to open our eyes to the real world. I feel that for us, we have gone through what most do not experience in a lifetime, and we are smart enough to learn and grow with each experience.

Our love for each other is deep and strong. I will never forget after each surgery, (there were many) just the touch and warmth of his hand holding mine, always gave me a certain peace. I have had so many surgeries and have been in the hospital so much that his warm touch is the one thing that I looked forward to as I woke in pain from a drug-induced slumber.

Throughout my disease, he has been relentless in searching for a cure. He is the one who started the research bug in me. He has literally spent hours and hours on the Internet researching any possible vitamins, diets, or cures that could help me. When people hear what I have been through, they think that it has been horrible for me, but, it has been harder on my family. My husband has had to watch his feisty wife go from bouncy and energetic, to gravely ill. Over the years, he has watched and cared for me gallantly. When I was first diagnosed with Crohn's disease, I ballooned in weight from the high doses of steroids that the doctors were pumping into my body. I thought for sure that he would leave me. How could anyone love such an ugly person, as I thought I had become? I, for the first time in my life, noticed how people looked at me differently. They treated me differently. It was as if my ugliness was going to rub off on them. It is very true that most people judge you on beauty. Some would recognize the prednisone look, and would instantly have pity fill their eyes. Others just looked at me as if I were a fat pig.

My husband stuck it through and surprised me completely. He is my air, my very breath. I love and admire him so much. I'm sure that I would have given up on life long ago if it was not for him and our love. It has to be rough for your family to watch you whittle away and teeter on death's porch. My family and friends are able to plainly see the changes in me. Now it is up to us to make the most of it. Our new life is just starting! It's up to us to make a difference—to start a revolution of sorts and build better, healthier communities! Yes, saving the world *is* possible! Not one person can ever tell me ever again that something is not possible! **Anything is possible! Never give up!! Push, push, push!** On *anything* you want to accomplish—there is a solution to every problem. There is always a way—just be patient and it will happen, even if only in baby steps, but it will happen! Self sought after knowledge, personal research, and keeping all your ideas on paper will allow you to find the truth and find a way to be free!

CHAPTER 3

I have always been a very prideful person. Over the years, I have hidden my sickness from others well. I toughed it out during my job managing a bar. The moment when I was not sure I could count on myself, I planned to step down. I took a bank job thinking that it would be better for my health ... but I was wrong. I had never been an untrustworthy employee, and by that I mean, calling in sick, and missing work often. I found myself getting more and more sick, eventually leaving the workforce completely.

Now climbing out from this **HELL** I am more excited than ever to get back to work as soon as I am able. Writing a book is the only thing I keep thinking about. It makes me feel useful to think that I may finally be helpful in bringing money in our household once again—helping to lift the financial burden that my sickness has caused, from my husband.

As a kid, I was a hard-core tomboy. I was proud to challenge any boy to any task and win or come close; brandishing any cut or bruises as proud battle wounds. In high school, I got into the sport of power lifting. Winning several state gold, silver, and bronze medals. I had one hell of a body, I just never realized it. LOL! My high school experience really was a good one. I had a high school sweetheart for almost four years and graduated in mediocrity early at semester.

During adolescence, I struggled with tonsillitis and missed a ton of school because of it. At the age of sixteen, I had them taken out. That was my first experience with a hospital. Later that same year, I had severe stomach pain and had my boyfriend at the time take me to the emergency room. I thought I had appendicitis; the pain was unbearable, bringing me to my knees. At the hospital, they informed me I was just having painful ovulation. They gave me a huge amount of pain medication and I don't even remember anything until the next day.

That right there should have been the first red flag, to pop up for me. That, now more than ever, tells me that even the doctors with all of their experience, knowledge, and schooling, are only guessing in the end. I mean, come on! Like my eggs are reaching out and digging claws into my fallopian tubes as they fall down to the uterus, screaming "No, I don't want to go!" causing that much pain? Give me a break!!

CHAPTER 4

After graduation, my high school sweetheart and I parted ways and I met my husband. After working, drinking, and partying for a little less than a year, I was pregnant with my first child. I was eighteen years old and was sent to live with my grandparents during my pregnancy while my future husband enrolled in college to better himself to support his new family. I will always cherish that experience—being able to live and grow close to my grandparents was a great and wonderful thing for me.

My grandpa, now gone, I am truly grateful I was able to know him. He could have been saved by the oil as well, (which I will explain later) and died very young at the age of sixty-three from lung cancer, or the radiation, It was painful for him nonetheless. My grandparents lived in a very small community in northern Kansas and had only two doctors for the area. The year was 1995 and the entire community was lit on fire by the fact that a phone company finally brought lines to the town and ended the community party lines. You would actually have to pick up the phone to make sure that your neighbor was not on before you made a call and you had to remember that your neighbors listened in on your conversations as well. Five houses shared the same party line and would have to use the honor system and wait for a neighbor to finish their call before you could make your own. If you had an emergency, you would just pick it up and tell them to get off to call for help.

My pregnancy went well with no problems until delivery. I woke up at three o'clock in the morning thinking I was wetting the bed; only to find my water had broken. My grandma was unable to find a replacement for her job and still had to go in. She had a management position at the hospital and would be able to pop in and out. We had to call my aunt at five o'clock to ask her to take me to the hospital. I was so amazed by how calm they both were! They kept telling me to be prepared and that it was going to take hours with it being my first child. Panic set in—didn't they know I was in labor!? That was all I could think! I paced the floor and waited from three until five o'clock. The panicking got worse when my aunt showed up about seven o'clock. When we arrived at the hospital around eight, I was already dilated to three centimeters. Within hours, my future husband, my mother, and my sister arrived. I asked for pain medication and they gave me a shot of something, but it could have just been saline because it didn't touch my pain at all.

By the time I was able to get another shot of pain medicine, it was too late. I was denied because I had already dilated to ten centimeters. I could feel the baby moving down the birth canal, stretching and burning as the baby moved down. He came down facing the wrong way and you could touch the hair on his head. Each time I pushed, he would crown and I would take a breath and he slipped right back in. We did this for four hours. My grandma, having worked at that hospital for years, was very adamant about not using forceps to help the child out. I don't think that they had a great track record using those tools. The doctor decided to insert his entire **GINOURMOUS** hand into my vagina and grab a hold of the baby's head; to turn it no less!

The pain made me scream profanities at the doctor. After he tried at least a half a dozen times, I was exhausted. They called an anesthesiologist and he flew on a jet to get ready to perform an emergency c-section. By the time they started to prep for the surgery and lifted me onto a cold metal table, my body was involuntarily trying to push the baby out. I was lying on my side with five men holding me down as I heaved in a ball and relaxed and heaved and relaxed. They were holding me and trying to keep me still to insert an epidural into my spinal column. By the time the medication kicked in, the doctors went into high gear. They put my butt in the air as I laid on my back and they shoved that baby back up my birth canal—elbow deep I might add. They did this to put the baby back to perform a "safe" c-section.

They refused to let my future husband in the room, because it was hospital policy… they said, we were not yet married. He was able to watch through a small window. They got the baby out at 4:28 P.M. and he did not cry, so they wheeled him off. All I was able to see was the top of his little nose as he was whisked out of the room. He had a bad case of jaundice, but other than that he was fine. We both stayed for about a week and we took our healthy baby boy home on the same day I was released.

CHAPTER 5

We ended up moving back to southwest Kansas and struggled as a new family. By the time our oldest was two, we were thinking of expanding our family—even though we couldn't afford it. We had no luck however. I was having abdominal pain once again and went to the doctor to find I had endometriosis. I was told that a pregnancy may reverse the endometriosis and we started on fertility drugs. At the same time, we were climbing out of poverty, saving money, fixing our credit, purchasing a new car, getting married, and finally trying to purchase a new home. We found a home and the owner allowed us to rent it until the paperwork was finalized. At the same time, my gynecologist decided it would be best to remove the scar tissue from the area in order to better house a child. The year was 2000—the new millennium! The entire world was excited and cautious all at the same time at what this new era would bring.

The week before the big move, I had a laparoscopic surgery that was not supposed to take very long—twenty or thirty minutes was all it was expected to take for this "routine" procedure. When I woke, I was told it had taken hours. The doctor was not sure why, but my insides were stuck in strange places due to the amount of scar tissue. Ovaries stuck to my bladder and abdominal wall and fallopian tubes stuck to ovaries. He said it was a mess in there and he hoped he put everything back so that we could continue to try for a child. He had also commented on how surprised he was by the fact that I had not complained any sooner about the pain. "It couldn't have been fun with that mess," he had told me.

Three days after I was released from the hospital, I was moving to our new home, lifting and moving things I was forbidden to do by the doctor. *I was tough, I was going to be just fine*, I thought. Around this time, one of my husband's cousins, was (and still is) in dire need of a kidney. Her own family was overweight and unable to donate. I thought that was ridiculous! If someone in my family was dying and needed a kidney, if I needed to lose a large amount of weight—I would have made sure to do it. Going to have my teeth wired shut if necessary … it's family, you do what you need to, right?

So I went and found out my blood type to see if it would match hers. I called her up and we took classes. I was willing to give her one of my kidneys to save her life despite constant scrutiny by family and friends. My gynecologist suggested that I wait at least until I have another child to donate the kidney. My husband and I discussed it and decided to break the news to his cousin. We were going to try for another child first and then donate the kidney. I felt horrible and selfish, but I desperately wanted another child. We didn't think it would take very long at all.

My grandpa got sick, and his doctor found stage-four lung cancer throughout his body. They put him on radiation, but he went from bad to worse and was gone within the year. He passed on New Year's Day 2002. At the end of that month, my husband and I went to a wedding of a good friend of ours that was out of town. My husband was a groomsman, and on the night of the wedding, we went to a local restaurant to enjoy ourselves with supper and drinks for the reception.

I, a well-seasoned bartender, tried one of their margaritas. I can't stand tequila since it made me sick as a teenager. This however was—and still is—the best margarita I've ever tasted. They were served in small rocks glasses with salt around the rim. In two-hours plus a meal, I consumed three of these drinks.

For the wedding, I had put on a slimming undergarment. I was losing my figure, but not gaining any weight (which was very confusing at the time). I have since come to the conclusion that this was just the beginning of scar tissue inhibiting my abdominal cavity. My body was starting to lose its hourglass figure and started to look more like a hot dog. … So, I used the sliming undergarment that day, and after my third margarita, I was in the restroom vomiting, and taking the undergarment off at the restaurant. Soon after, I snuck outside and sat in the car with the door wide open, puking in the gutter for about three hours. For the first two hours, the vomiting felt non-stop. The nausea persisted in the last hour, but the physical emesis had finally ceased.

My husband kept coming out to check on me, and so did others. I told them all that I was fine—when I knew I was not. I told them all that I had had too much to drink. We were there to celebrate a new couple starting a new life, and I was not about to take the limelight away from their new beginning. I knew something was very wrong. I was not drunk by any means, and the pain in my stomach was worse than labor contractions. As the evening wore on, I was starting to get scared. The pain was very intense and was getting harder to hide that fact from the others.

I knew it was bad, and when the restaurant closed up for the evening, I almost had my husband take me to an emergency room, but it was more than an hour away. We were traveling and not familiar with the area. I decided to deal with the pain and wait to see what the next day would bring. When we got back, I made an appointment with my doctor. They had found that a very large cyst had formed on one of my ovaries, and had burst on its own. This, I thought explained everything away until two weeks later, and I was in pain again, doubled over and heading to the ER. My previous history of "painful ovulation" was explained, and laughed at, as we all concluded it was appendicitis. I went in for immediate surgery and woke up later in the hospital.

CHAPTER 6

My whole family was there when I woke up. My husband lovingly cared for me and never stopped holding my hand to give me comfort. I could feel the warmth of his hand spread through my cold body, like a warm blanket of love, calm and peace. My family doctor arrived with the surgeon and an apprentice. My family doctor, who has cared for me from the time I was five years old, was sitting at the foot of my bed. The surgeon explained that, when they had started the surgery, so much fluid was left in my abdomen from the massive cyst that had popped two weeks before that they had to remove the liquid before they could start.

While removal was underway, they had noticed signs on my bowels of Crohn's disease. They had decided to take out my appendix, even though its functionality was just fine. Appendicitis and Crohn's disease have almost the exact same symptoms and severity in pain. To remove it now would cause less confusion in the future. At that time, I was speechless. My mind couldn't focus on anything other than the words "Crohn's disease." I was in shock. My first question was "How long do I have left?" The apprentice said, "Ten, maybe twelve years … if you're lucky.", as he has his stethoscope to my tummy.

My family doctor gave him the evil eye and the surgeons left the room. He sat and explained Crohn's disease to me with tears in his eyes. He told me that it was a very rare, horrible, and painful disease, that I had a long road ahead of me, and that he was truly sorry. Over the next couple of days in the hospital, as the doctors and the nurses came in and out, we picked their brains on this so-called "rare disease." Our research continued at home on the Internet. At that time, the information on this disease was hard to come by.

So, essentially what is Crohn's disease, you may ask? Well, I usually start off by telling people that God himself sat back …thought for a moment, … and said, "What's the worst- ASS disease I can come up with to give to Shona? … Crohn's! LOL! Crohn's disease is an autoimmune disease. I try to explain that it is kind of the opposite of HIV or AIDS. In AIDS, (which is also an autoimmune disease), patient's their immune system is almost nonexistent, exposing their bodies more easily to illness and disease; which can sometimes lead to their demise.

Crohn's disease, however, is not contracted or spread from person to person. It is also incurable according to the medical community. Crohn's has an unknown origin, and there are many different theories on how it is contracted. Some believe it is in your genes like cancer. Others believe it is our environment and the things that we eat; while others believe it is caused by bacteria in the bowels … For me I think it has to do with all of the above, with a spin of government-controlled evolution, of which I will go into further later on.

Crohn's disease, as I said, is opposite to AIDS. In Crohn's, the body's immune system is in overdrive, recognizing that something is not quite right and attacking itself in the process of trying to find the problem. It affects the entire digestive system—from your mouth to your anus—and will become irritated and inflamed. In my case, Crohn's started out as severe inflammation, causing swelling, pain, and complete blockage of my bowels at times. Toward the end of the disease, the terminal stages of the disease, the body is unable to absorb nutrition, and whatever you put in your body shoots through the other end as fast as it can, causing on some occasions a bowel movement just five to ten minutes after eating. This causes severe weight loss, eventually your body starves to death and you can even feel the body trying to feed off of the muscle when all of the fat has been depleted. It feels as if you have a constant stomach flu or a really bad case of food poisoning that comes with horrendous cramping, diarrhea, and nausea with a touch of occasional vomiting as well—all of the time!

A normal person with the stomach flu can look forward to the end of it knowing it will only last a week—maybe two if it is severe—but you know it will eventually run its course. With Crohn's, there is no relief. It takes everything out of you. If you would like to see with your own eyes what it is like, I encourage you to watch an amazing video on YouTube that describes it the best. It is a clip from the movie *Dumb and Dumberer* called "The Bathroom Scene." Put that in the YouTube search engine and you will see a five-minute clip that will make you laugh until you cry! A fantastic example of what I went through *every day* for eight years with sometimes as many as fifty plus trips to the lavatory in one day! If you want to further an Internet search at this time, select images on any search engine and type out Crohn's disease. This, however, is not for the squeamish, so you are forewarned.

Now, back to the story …

On my six-week check up after surgery, my family doctor informed me that this disease was just out of his league, and he referred me to a specialist in Amarillo Texas. We went to see the gastroenterologist to discuss our options; the pain was still present and not improving. A colonoscopy was scheduled, and my mother-in-law accompanied me to Amarillo. The procedure itself was to be painless, the prep however, was going to be tough, I was told. I was handed an entire gallon of this stuff called Co-Lite, I had to drink the entire thing to clean out my bowels. I'm not sure what was worse … it going down or it exploding out the other end. I went from toilet to bath to toilet to bath and, hours later, exhausted, fell asleep to go in early for the procedure.

I woke in the recovery room screaming from the unbearable, sharp cramping pain. The nurses did not know what to do. They got me off the bed and carried me under each arm to walk me up and down the hall to no avail. They were finally given a green light by the doctor to give me pain medication. I woke in the middle of the night from a burning pain and the sound and feel of my skull cracking. I opened my eyes to scream out, because my voice couldn't make a sound. I had seen two nurses back away quickly. One was teaching the other how to insert a nasal gastric tube. This tube runs down your nose through your esophagus and down to the stomach to prevent vomiting by not allowing any content into the stomach. The new nurse was pointing the sharp end that looked like the end of a juice box straw (only much larger) straight back to my skull without guiding it in and down the esophagus. The more experienced nurse told her to just push harder as my skull started to crack again. I was able to grunt and shake a big "no" with my finger, took out the tube, and handed it to the other nurse to finish the job.

When I woke the next day, I couldn't speak. My throat was like raw hamburger. The specialist explained that I had a blockage, which the scope had irritated, causing the swelling to inflame tenfold. After three days, I was allowed to go home and put on several medications. Prednisone, Pentasa, Imuran, Sulfa, antibiotics, and more that I can't even remember. At that time, I was taking forty-eight pills a day. Nothing was working. This went on for months … gaining weight, around thirty pounds from the prednisone. The pain and bloating would not alleviate. I would go days without having a stool, and the Prednisone just made me eat more than I ever needed. This resulted in such severe bloating that I sported old maternity clothing. During that time, on any given day, I looked between six and eight months pregnant.

CHAPTER 7

The nausea was relentless, the bloating was unbearable, and when I puked (which was often) the cramping in my bowels only got extremely worse. During one of my many trips to pray to the porcelain god, my husband was holding back my hair as he begged me to try marijuana. He explained that I had the same symptoms as cancer patients, if it helps them, why not try it? At that point, I was ready to try anything! I was absolutely miserable. He brought me some and had to show me how to smoke it. Within seconds, the pain, nausea, and cramping had started to subside. It was absolutely amazing! I remember crying because this simple little plant was not the scary drug that I was taught that it was! This helped much better than any pain pill I had taken. The nausea was gone completely and the cramping was not so intense. In the beginning, I would roll a joint and take small amounts of it at night. It was not until I had my hysterectomy later in life that I started an all-day regimen.

For many years, I had considered myself a "pothead." I put the same stereotype that many have onto myself. I felt naughty—and even dirty—for breaking the law. It was not until I watched the movie "Run from the Cure" that I realized that I was one of those people. I could benefit even more from this plant. I started to look at myself as a medical marijuana patient. It opened my eyes to the system and I started to think, know, and realize that I needed to take my life into my own hands in order to get better.

Over the years, I found it easier to be honest with my children about my marijuana use. At first I tried to hide it, but when my oldest was old enough to ask and get curious about it, we educated him at the same time we were educating ourselves. If a documentary about the plant was on the television, we watched it as a family. I would research the subject on the Internet and share what I learned with my husband and child over dinner. We had all learned that this plant was "safe" and it was the healthiest substance on the government's drug list. We found out that this plant has fewer side effects than aspirin, had antibacterial/antimicrobial properties, relieved pain, and eliminated nausea. Since 1974, our government has known that the concentrated THC in this plant had been proven to not only kill abnormal cells in the body that cause cancer and other ailments and that it does so in a way that does not damage healthy cells around them. On the contrary, the concentrated THC actually restores and regenerates cell growth. The government has known this for longer than I have been alive. It is a proven fact it has never caused death by overdose. My husband and I feel that being honest and forthcoming with our children is the best parenting we can give them—anything less would be negligent on our part.

I was completely honest with the gastroenterologist from the start. I asked him about it on the very next visit. He was very vague, … saying that—by law—he was unable to confirm or deny any claims made by other patients, but that he had many patients with Crohn's disease that used that substance. He left it at that. I went to have more X-rays, and he concluded that none of the drugs he had prescribed were working. Surgery was our best course of action; within two weeks, we had an appointment with a surgeon.

CHAPTER 8

The plan was to remove the half-inch of bowel between my large and small intestines, trying to keep my ileum intact if possible. Upon meeting with the surgeon he felt that the procedure needed to be done as soon as possible, and he moved the surgery up a full day. After the appointment, we met up with the hospital's "Pain Management Team" and the surgeon strongly suggested that I have an epidural along with a morphine drip. At the office, I had explained my previous problems with nerve damage from an epidural with the c-section of my son. This had given me back problems and a numb strip of skin on my right thigh that was about an inch and a half wide and stretched on the outer side of my thigh from my knee to my hip. During the hour of discussion, I let them know about my previous experiences with pain medication, morphine makes me vomit, itch, and be confused. Demerol was the only other pain medication that I had received during a hospital stay, it would make me nauseated but would control the pain better than the morphine with fewer side effects to my personal body. The "Pain Management Team" insisted that, with the epidural in place, I would have the best pain management. The epidural was to stay lodged in my spine for the entire duration of my recovery, but they wanted me to try it. I was told that if I had any problems, I should let them know and I could go to a more familiar pain medication such as Demerol.

My gastroenterologist had scheduled X-rays the next day. After they were done, I was to start my bowel prep once again by drinking that nasty gallon of Co-Lite. During the X-rays, the radiologist administered a heavy, chalky, metal-tasting stuff they try to hide with fruity flavor.... Barium, this illuminated the bowels as they took the X-ray. For these tests, I had an X-ray every fifteen minutes and then every thirty minutes and then every hour, for six hours. The barium hurt so bad moving through my bowels, and the pain at the blockage only got worse as the day progressed, making me almost look forward to cleaning out my bowels.

That evening, I started my bowel prep with the nasty gallon of crap I had to drink. My husband and I stayed in a hotel near the hospital, and the prep was painful. I was vomiting the drink, trying hard to keep it down. The cramping and pain only worsened as the night wore on. I was unable to get any rest, I woke my husband early the next morning around 4:00. The surgery was scheduled for 7:00, but the pain was so intense that my body felt an urgency I had never felt before. I knew that if I did not get help very soon, I would die.

We arrived at the hospital at five o'clock in the morning. I was in so much pain that I had doubled over, crying uncontrollably, and started to hyperventilate. I was wheeled into a room after much begging to the hospital staff, who were very confused about why I came in two hours early for a procedure and why I was in so much pain. I did not have those answers; I was in pain, and that was as far as my brain would allow me to think. It felt as if it was an eternity before I was relieved of that pain. Not long after, more staff came to prep me for surgery. When I woke from the surgery, I was told that there were complications during the procedure. The surgeon, instead of taking out the half of an inch as expected, was forced to remove **one foot** of my small intestine, **my ileum**, and **half of my colon** because of the barium. The barium was unable to leave my body because the blockage had just swelled shut. This allowed the barium to dry up like concrete and very literally killed **eighteen inches** of intestine—but that's okay, right? God gave us twenty-two feet of small intestine and a whole twelve inches of large intestine, (also known as the colon) to start out life with. I had plenty left, and it was my new goal to have the tightest sphincter muscles in the state, to fill in for the loss of my ileum. I tried very hard to always look at the bright side and face this thing with fists flailing (rhetorically speaking). I always tried to bring humor to the plate. One of the things I'm known for in the hospital over the years is the fact that whenever anyone entered my room, cartoons would be on the television. I have always been teased lightly for it, but I always try to explain that it's almost impossible to get depressed when you watch Bugs Bunny and Elmer Fudd go at it.

No matter what I tried that night, the overwhelming pain would not subside. I remember the nurses yelling at me to breathe slowly and to calm down, at one time grabbing me by my shoulders and shaking me, screaming in my face to shut up. Please remember that this was a pretty serious surgery and that I was cut from my sternum to my pelvis in a vertical fashion. I was held together with glue and staples, begging the nurse to believe me that the epidural was apparently not working. I was assured that it was working fine and should not be in pain, that it was all in my head. For the next several days, the pain persisted. I would say that I called for pain and was yelled at for it five to ten times per day. By day three, during another painful episode, the same violent nurse from before came in yelling at me telling me that three days after a surgery you should not be in pain and should be healing just fine! She was stomping around the room and throwing open the curtains like a madwoman. She told me that I was just faking the entire thing! That was it for me! I called different areas of the hospital before I finally was able to talk to someone on the "Pain Management Team" personally. I had found that not one nurse had spoken to them about the situation. They agreed that the epidural was apparently not working and came right up to my room to take it out and replace the morphine drip with Demerol— ... and it was *sooo* much better! I had relief for one afternoon and was able to sleep most of the evening for the first time and finally started to relax.

The very next morning, the same violent nurse came in and removed my IV, took me off the Demerol, and put me on Darvocet pills—the lowest dose narcotic pill that they offer. At the time, it had the same effect as if I had taken a Flintstones vitamin for the pain. It was absolute hell for the next two days! I laid there in my bed, in a fetal position crying in pain. I asked for a doctor or a nurse, but I never got an answer. The nurses shut my door and only opened it to give me food or let in an aide to take my vitals.

On the day of my dismissal, my gastroenterologist, the surgeon, and staff that looked as if they came from the entire floor. I did not recognize most of the ten to fifteen people in my room. They informed me that I was addicted to narcotics and that I was being sent home. They gave a long spiel that lasted about five minutes. I don't remember much of what they said—I was so shocked that they would accuse me of being a narcotics addict one week after such an invasive, and serious surgery. To top it off, how could they assume that I would heal quickly? I was still on very heavy doses of steroids (an immune-suppressing drug), heavy doses of Imuran (also an immune-suppressing drug), and it is even taught in nursing school that if pain is present, it takes longer for the body to heal itself. They told me that they had come to the conclusion that I was an addict because the nurse had said that on one occasion, I had pretended to fall asleep after being given a Darvocet pill. ... and that is when I remember being in so much pain and waiting for pain medication that I popped the pill in my mouth and swallowed, trying to ignore her outburst, as she was angry that I had called the pain management team over her head. I closed my eyes and ignored her, pretending to be asleep as she stormed and yelled about in the room. ... At that point, there was nothing left in me to fight. I was released on a Thursday and remember second-guessing myself. Maybe I was just overreacting; maybe the pain really was all in my head. ... The weekend proved me to be very wrong.

CHAPTER 9

First thing Monday morning, I was in to see my family doctor. I was in so much pain and let him know that I thought something was wrong. He prescribed some pain medication, gave me an examination, and told me I needed to go home to get some much-needed rest.

Now at this time, we had family and friends staying with us. The economy was slow, and my house was constantly full of people in need of a roof. We had eight people living under one roof, and my husband was the only one working and bringing in any income. Because of that stress alone, I had played off the disease to my husband, not letting him know how serious it was, trying to hide my pain from him and my child.

I remember being home for two weeks, still in pain. I knew something was seriously wrong with me, and I felt my body worsen day by day. I went to my local emergency room nine ... yes, **NINE** times in that two-week period. Each time, I was sent home crying because I left with the feeling that it was once again all in my head and I was just overreacting.

After about visit number seven, I decided that I needed to get my final affairs in order. I actually got out a phone book and called funeral homes to price check packages and costs for caskets and so forth. I wanted to take care of as much as I could before I ran out of time and take that responsibility lovingly away from my husband—all the while keeping it a secret to myself.

One day, I was lying in my recliner and my friend looked at me and asked if I was okay. I confided in her that I was not, but I felt an urgency to do something or I was going to die. I felt impending doom and it was a heavy feeling deep within my heart. As I was speaking with her, I reclined in my chair, my eyes kept rolling to the back of my head, and it was getting harder for me to finish my sentences and concentrate. I was fighting with all I had to stay awake! My friend recognized something was very wrong and called to speak to my local surgeon who had found my Crohn's disease to begin with when he had given me the appendectomy only months before.

I don't remember what exactly was said, but I do look back and laugh a little because this gal was downright scary when she was pissed ... and she was pissed! LOL! She *informed* him that he would meet us at the local emergency room and he would examine me personally. He apparently complied, as he was there when we arrived. I did not even have to wait—the staff was expecting me. As soon as we went into an examination room, he was waiting to see me.

The old man took one look at me and instantly knew something was wrong. I felt warm but had no fever. They ran blood work, but it always came back fine. He said my color was off, and anyone with eyes could see that I was sick. He was so upset with the test results that he had more done on a daily basis and sent them to different labs around the state.

I was very scared. I knew I was on a slippery slope and was at the mercy of my local physicians. He gave me as much pain medication as I needed, and I was able to wean myself off at my own pace with no problems by the time I was released. He recognized that I was fighting some sort of infection, he was just unable to put his finger on it. He ordered a central line put in because my veins would blow after just a few days and had started to roll and hide from the nurses while they poked and dug for any vein they could use for an I.V.

A central line is a line that they insert just underneath your collarbone. They must use a scalpel, but are able to perform the procedure in the patient's room with a local anesthetic. This line is connected with one of the major veins to the heart, and doctors are able to put three ports leading off of one line—allowing the patient access to more intravenous medication. I was given a T.P.N. for nutrition (liquid food), and they started me on a very powerful antibiotic called Cipro. That name may sound familiar because it was widely used for those who had come in contact with anthrax years ago. The old man kept in touch on a daily basis with the Gastro in Amarillo, letting him know about my condition and my recovery. I gradually got better and was released.

CHAPTER 10

After being home and recovering for a week ... I got a phone call from my state health department, informing me that my test results came back positive for, E. coli, Campylobacter, and Cholestrum Difficial (also known as C-Diff). My first question was why the health department was calling me instead of my doctor. They informed me that they were required by law to inform anyone who tests positive for the E. coli bacteria. They then informed me that I was very lucky to have survived such an infection, which included these three very dangerous strains of bacteria.

Immediately after the phone call, I called my doctor in Amarillo. I informed him of what the health department had told me. I also explained that my husband had a theory that my stay under his care was the core cause of the infection, as I had spent days in a fetal position, every muscle in my body involuntarily tense from the pain, my face swollen in tears, begging for anyone to help me. During that time of trying to heal after resecting my bowels back together, the tensing had to have caused some kind of leak or tear in the newly resected section. E. coli is essentially fecal matter—how else would this have occurred? The gastro informed me that it was just probably food that I had eaten or prepared for my family at home. He told me that there were many different strains of E. coli out there—only one strain that was deadly—and I was overreacting again and should just let it go. He told me to call the health department to find the exact the strain to ease my mind and to call him back with the information.

The woman at the health department was furious when I explained my situation and let her know what the gastro had told me. She had said that yes, it was a deadly strain called E. coli 0157–H7. She also reminded me of the other bacteria and told me that—with my history and illness—I was lucky to be alive. I called the gastro back to inform him of the deadly strain and… the line was silent. I also told him that my stomach cramping was still an issue, and I wanted to know what was wrong. He then explained that, as far as he was concerned, this was the surgeon's fault and that it was the surgeon's call as to how my pain medication was treated. He also informed me that my body was just sensitive from the surgery and that my Crohn's had been completely removed; and therefore I may have irritable bowel syndrome as a result of the trauma from the surgery.

As far as I was concerned, this man was no longer a physician in my eyes… He was just a chicken shit trying to pass the buck on a serious situation… it was at that time, I finally stood up for myself and fired him as my gastroenterologist. I decided to take my chances and stick out my recovery and any further problems with my family doctor.

CHAPTER 11

My family doctor retired and I was able to find a new one within the same practice. We were able to control my bowel movements with a drug called Amitriptyline, it is supposed to be used for depression and a major side effect was severe constipation. This allowed me to have less than ten bowel movements a day. I was able to go on with my life for several months... smoking cannabis for my nausea and nominal cramping.In 2003, I was finally pregnant. My oldest child was six years old at the time and our entire family was very excited. We had wanted this child very badly, and I knew as the months wore on that it was the girl we had always hoped for. We had prepared her room and I even hand-made some bedding for her basinet. At this time we had no house guests and we were in a good family groove.During the pregnancy I had stopped my use of cannabis. I did indeed research the subject of using this drug while pregnant, to find out just how safe, or unsafe, it might be. There was not much that I could find...to say the least. It however confused me to find all personal accounts of women who consumed this plant while pregnant, had only good things to say about the effects that helped with nausea and helped them if they had any problems trying to eat. I also looked at other perspectives of physicians. I found that the only detrimental effect from this drug was the *possibility* of low birth weight and prematurity. In all, it was the same verbiage used to describe the effects of cigarette smoking on an unborn fetus. I did not want to take chances and decided to play it safe.

I was just ending my fourth month when I had severe stomach pain that once again brought me to my knees. I went in to the emergency room and refused X-rays because of the pregnancy. My previous surgeon had also retired at this point. His apprentice had taken over the position. He came in on a Saturday evening and explained that a surgery needed to be performed as soon as possible. My thoughts were that if he wanted to do this at six o'clock on a Sunday morning… then it must be important. The new surgeon went in the next day and did an exploratory surgery monitoring the baby the entire time. When I woke I felt something was not quite right with the baby. The monitors said that she was fine and both my surgeon and my OBGYN assured me that the baby seemed strong and made it through the surgery fine. The surgeon then informed me that he was a little unsure of my Crohn's disease diagnoses. He said that he had seen absolutely no signs of Crohn's disease, that it was scar tissue wrapping around my intestines and growing like vine completely restricting by bowels in many different areas. He had said that he had to take all of my intestines out of my body, laid them on my chest, and go through them and remove the scar tissue like a fine-toothed comb. He went inch by inch and said that it was so severe… I may need to have it done again in three to five years. I stayed in the hospital for two weeks on IV medication, and was released home with Tylenol-3 for the pain. I am allergic to the Codeine in that drug, it makes me vomit almost immediately, but my OBGYN was too afraid to give me anything stronger. The first night I was home with a brand new vertical scar from my sternum to my pelvis, I had lain down to try to sleep. I was in a lot of pain and still worried about the baby. I had some slight spotting of blood and was getting scared we might lose her. I was in agony. I got up from bed and tried to find a comfortable position on the couch. That was not working, so I moved to the recliner after a few hours. That did not work either, I remember crawling on all-fours, just trying to find any position that might give me relief. I had looked at the clock and it was almost six in the morning… the night was almost over. Upon opening my eyes again I was astonished to find that I was still in my own bed and only one hour had passed. It was one of the worst nightmares I have ever had in my lifetime! I'll never forget how *real* it was… the pain I had to endure after that surgery… will always be one of the hardest bouts I had to go through. I demanded an ultra-sound to be done after I was home from the hospital. The procedure had taken more than an hour to complete. The technician would not comment on anything. I was asking questions right and left. I could notice her little infant hands wide open and straight. I could see that her feet were tilted inward at the ankle and realized that this was what was called "clubbed feet"… we can fix that, I had thought. I was talking to a robot, he would not comment, talk, or answer any of my questions. It was so hard not to scream out and slap the man, I could clearly see something was wrong and I was only receiving silence… pure torture.

I soon had an appointment with the OBGYN and he was able to explain that she had hydrocephilitis, which is water on the brain. He explained that it was more common than I thought. The odds are one in one-hundred pregnancies that have this happen. He wanted me to go to a larger city to get a much better sonogram. The appointment was a full week away… that entire week I was in limbo. My body and mind were numb; I was completely lost in a deep depression.

In the city, after a high-tech sonogram, we were told that her condition was severe I could try to carry her to term with the possibility of being able to hold her for twenty or thirty minutes before she would pass away, or have a very slight chance that she may live eight to ten years, only as a bed-ridden vegetable. At this point, she only had enough tissue at the base of her neck to keep her heart pumping and any brain function was non-existent.

I had made the decision to terminate the pregnancy. For one… How can anyone carry a child for three more months when you know in your heart she was already gone? Two… My spotting continued, and because of the recent surgery, I was unsure if I could even miscarry this child on my own. The procedure took an entire week with me having to deliver her under a physicians care on a Friday morning.

This time in my life was one of the darkest for me. Our whole family unit was hurt by the loss. I was forced to step back and look at the situation. This wonderful child saved my life! If I would have gone into the hospital, without her, they would have had their X-rays and because you cannot see scar tissue on an X-ray, I would have been sent home to die. It is because of her that I am alive! I was also able to come to the conclusion that she, or her soul, had left during the surgery because of the feeling that I had of something not right when I had awakened from the procedure. It was all meant to be, and knowing that she was a gift from God that came down to save me is the greatest solace God himself has ever given me.

I never lost faith, but from this point until years later, God and I had an understanding. I was angry with him, I had gone through enough! Folks would constantly tell me "God is only giving you what you can handle; you are a strong woman." I don't know how many times or how many people gave me spiritual advice, or told me of bible stories. One story that would almost always get brought up was the story of Job. How God took everything from him, his loved ones and his possessions, to see if his faith would hold. I never stopped loving God... it was most comparable to when I am arguing with my husband. I can get so mad, so angry, and so hurt at times from him during our arguments, but my love never goes away.

I had two theories... That I had to have done something severely horrible in a past life that I was currently being punished for; or that before my soul came to this earth, before I was even born, maybe I went right up to God and challenged him. Maybe I told him that I wanted to experience all aspects of life, to learn everything I can. Maybe I said to him, give me all you got and I will do it. Give me the worst of the worst and then best of the best; I want to take it all on! Like I said, I really do believe this was all meant to be and I knew this was another lesson, all be it a hard one, that I needed to endure to help me later in life.

CHAPTER 12

Just two weeks after our loss, I was in our local Wal-Mart shopping for groceries and was approached by a woman of whom I used to work with. She was opening a new restaurant in town and wanted to know if I would help her out and work for her. This was a new door opening up for me and I knew I needed to keep myself busy in order to not be depressed, so I jumped at the chance.

After only two months of working, I found I was pregnant again and sent flowers to my husbands' employment to spring the good news on him. I continued to work as a manager in the restaurant until I was forced to go into bed rest by six months in. I had decided to continue with my cannabis use during this pregnancy to keep from vomiting, try to eat, and not add any undue agitation to this pregnancy. This time it was another boy and we were all so excited! The baby was very active in the womb and one day I had to call my OBGYN because it felt like he was trying to kick out through my cervix. The doc asked me to go in to the hospital; I asked to be put on magnesium to stop the labor. We had made it to thirty-three weeks and a full forty weeks is full term.

The baby was coming and he was determined so we all got ready for a c-section because he was completely breach. When they opened me up they found that not only was he breach, but the cord was wrapped around his little neck multiple times. I had to wait hours to see him in the neo-natal intensive care unit or the NICU. He had a glass house and was under a heat lamp with a plastic bowl looking piece of equipment over his head and face. He was three pounds and twelve ounces... so thin and tiny. His little ears were still stuck to his little head that was about the same size of a small orange.

We were only allowed to hold him three times a day for ten minute increments. That was torture. I had remembered something called kangaroo care, I still don't remember where I picked it up at, but I always knew if I ever was faced with a premature baby, that I would practice it. Kangaroo care is the act of placing a brand new naked baby on the naked chest of its parents, to help the child bond with the parent... skin on skin. I would go into the NICU and take off what I had from the waist up, I then had the nurse place my son on my chest and we would just rock. A little over a week went by and they started to allow me to teach him to breast feed. It was so hard to try to get him to latch on. The process took anywhere from three to seven minutes to just get him to learn to suckle, then the nurses would literally rip him from my breast because of the ten minute time limit, just as he was getting the hang of it.... I have still never understood that, still to this day, if only I had the balls to say something then... I may have been thrown in jail... you never know. It was all meant to be right?

My husband and I took video of him every day for my oldest son. The hospital would not let him into the NICU because of his age and an outbreak of RSV. We had to make our seven year old stay in the waiting room each and every time. Of course this **never** affected the staff... they would bring in their children to see the new babies in the room, and my son had to watch other children go in and out, unable to see his new baby brother. He was confused and upset often, it was heart wrenching to go through. Stupid rules and regulations only enforced on whom they choose.

I knew this needed to be my last child and the OBGYN was going to "tie my tubes" during the c-section, but I desperately wanted to make sure this little guy made it through. On my first visit in to the OBGYN for my check-up we scheduled a tubule ligation to be performed. The doctors' explicit instructions were to solder those suckers off and throw them away!

CHAPTER 13

After recovering from my eighth surgery at this point, I went back to work. Several months went by and life started to get back to "normal". Crohn's disease was not yet finished with me I'm afraid. I had started to get what they call "flare-ups". Pain would come on and I would take it for as long as I could. The cramping would start off light and progress, to mind numbingly severe. It would only subside at night after work when I allowed myself small hits or puffs off of a marijuana cigarette. Now, if by chance I was unable to find any of that particular medication, and a "flare-up" occurred, I was admitted in the hospital. The only way at that point to make it calm down was with high amounts of steroids, antibiotics, and pain medication.

While in the hospital, I was forced to be NPO. That is a medical term that means the patient is not allowed food or drink, period. This was a good thing, because on several occasions I was given an NG tube up my nose and down to my stomach. These things are just awful. On one particular visit to the hospital, I remember puking out the tube, being so sick and weak, having to have my husband bathe me. Even though it was my husband, the simple thing of not being strong enough to stand or bathe yourself in the hospital shower, it eats at your core.

Over the next few years I was able to continue and push on; In and out of the hospital every few months. There came a time when I knew I was getting worse. I was running a very busy and popular place of business and even though I loved every second of it my body was not able to keep up. A replacement was found and I stepped down. I had applied at a bank thinking a desk job would be easier on my body. I gave the impression I was decent at ten key entry and got the job. Over the next two weeks I downloaded a ten key typing tutor and practiced my tail off.

Taking it easy and sitting behind a desk is not such an easy task either. It was a HUGE culture shock to me. I went from running my tail off, to sitting and typing. It was just not for me. I stuck it through, losing weight and going back to my old hospital routine. My fat prednisone look was just finally going away and I was very excited … at first. The weight loss seemed to be persistent; I realized that it was from malnutrition, my body was unable to gain any weight no matter how much or how often I ate. Not long after my sudden loss of forty to fifty pounds in three to four months did I have sharp stabbing pain just below my sternum (my chest bone). I went to the doctor. He reluctantly ordered tests to be done because it was possible my gallbladder was malfunctioning.

Sure enough after the results came in it showed that my gallbladder had lost seventy percent of its function. There was no rhyme or reason for it to have stopped working. The surgeon had no answers for me except that… it just happens. I was concerned about worsening pain during my menstrual cycles. Each month my Crohn's would flare up and it was getting harder and harder for me to control. I knew he was going to put me under to take out my gallbladder, I was hoping he would be willing to take out my uterus at the same time. Knock out two birds with one stone right?

He had said he was not comfortable with performing both procedures at one time and told me that he was only concerned about my gallbladder for the time being. The surgery itself was a simple laparoscopic procedure and the stay in the hospital was short and sweet, compared to the several weeks I had become accustomed to. After the surgery he highly recommended me to see a professional Gastroenterologist once again and that meant a four hour drive to another large city. While I was in the clinic for my six week check up, I was wearing a sleeveless shirt and he looks at a bright red mole on my right arm. He actually grabbed my arm and looked very intently at it and told me he could easily remove it in the office and to make a quick appointment on the way out. He told me that he would like to have it biopsied just to be safe; which was totally fine with me. The ugly little thing started to grow when I was pregnant with my oldest child. I had never known exactly what it was, but it kept getting larger each year. Having a scar that would eventually fade away seemed much better than this nasty red dot that looked like an ugly pimple. It was set for just a few weeks later. I returned back to work at the bank, and I proudly went around showing off a photo of my gallbladder after the surgery. It looked like a brown gelatinous, slimy pile of mass… it was all mine. I made it. Taking the photo in to show others let them know that I took the surgery just fine and was going to be okay. I hate it when others worry. This was my way of easing their minds with a bit of shock humor.

CHAPTER 14

I made the appointment to see a new Gastroenterologist and my husband and I took the four hour drive to meet with him. He seemed to be very nice and sincere; it did seem like this man cared and understood more of what I was dealing with on a daily basis. More tests were ordered and colonoscopies were performed. He confirmed that yes indeed I had Crohn's disease because the surgeon at home was not convinced. He recommended that I start Remicade infusions.

Remicade is a very powerful and delicate drug made of artificial antibodies from lab mice. The nurses that administer this drug must treat it with special care. This drug is so temperamental that it must be kept in a cool refrigerator. When the nurse mixes the powder with a saline solution, she must gently swirl it to mix it. Shaking this drug or over agitating it can have detrimental effects. An I.V. must be established for the infusion to begin. The patient must be monitored very carefully; blood pressure must be checked every fifteen minutes for the three to four hours it takes to process the infusion. Remicade has about nine different side effects a patient must worry about... and seven of them are deadly.

The new Gastro was honest and up front about those side effects. At the same time he explained this was my best option to get relief from the constant pain in his opinion. I was to travel every eight weeks, four hours for the infusion and was to do this for ... the rest of my life. I was desperate for anything to work and help me out. He also explained that this treatment was most comparable to chemotherapy treatments with most of the same side effects; all but the hair loss, of which I was most grateful for. After each infusion I was completely drained of all energy. For the next three to four days after, I was bedridden, feeling like I got hit by a truck. Every muscle is weak beyond belief, nausea was another thing I had to go through during this so called recovery. When I could finally get out of bed, I did feel much better. My energy was up and I thought my life was going to turn around. I had even suggested this treatment for others that I knew had Crohn's disease.

Back at home, I went for my appointment for removal of the red mole on my arm. I was waiting in one of the examination rooms for the surgeon. He walked in and seemed to be surprised I was there. I told him that he wanted me to come in to remove the mole. He looked at me as if confused, then proceeded to tell me he said no such thing. Cautiously, he looked at the mole again, and was reluctant to remove it. He called in his nurse and she confirmed what I was trying to explain to him, that it was his request for this removal. He acted as if he were upset, or put out, that he had to do such a menial task. Then proceeded to tell me he was worried about my mental health on having so many surgeries. He had NEVER treated me with such distaste before! He removed the mole in the room and sent it off for testing. The results came back, it was found, thank goodness, that it was just a growth and was not cancerous in any way.

The surgeons' demeanor had really upset me, so much so that I confided in a friend in the medical field. He explained that flat out asking for a surgery will bring up a red flag for some in the medical community. Implying that I may be enjoying or "addicted" to surgery. He also explained that if this surgeon did not understand the final stages of Crohn's disease, he may have misunderstood my weight loss. The fact that I had had so many procedures and had been honest with my medical marijuana use, and now had lost a large amount of weight… it may have been easy for him to misconstrue the situation while looking at my chart and not remembering the person behind it. How on earth would this surgeon not know what this disease was capable of or what it had done to me? How can this man jump to such a conclusion? I had assumed he had become well versed in the disease and knew the implications thereof. I thought to myself, that if I were in his shoes, and had a patient with such an illness, and had taken care of that patient for several years… I would have researched the disease because I would have cared for that patient enough to do so.

That was my problem… I assumed that he had cared. I assumed that doctors were in their profession to care, and gravely realized that this man looked at his profession… as a paycheck. He looked at his patients as if they were cattle to be examined and pushed through a gate. I felt that from that moment on, I was no longer a patient, but a statistic. I had never asked for any previous procedure or surgery.

However, I did know my body and knew that with each menstrual cycle, my Crohn's would flare up, with each cramp, my bowels would scream. Each month would become worse and worse. It came to a point that even my natural green goodness would not alleviate my pain or symptoms, and then it came to a point that even after my cycle had run its course… my pain persisted and my bowels stayed in a constant tightness, a constant cramping.

CHAPTER 15

I waited as long as I possibly could, after three months of agony, even with the Remicade infusions, I could not take it any longer. I scheduled an appointment with my Gynecologist to find out what was wrong. I told him what was happening to my body, and **HE** suggested a hysterectomy. The plan was to remove my uterus and try to leave my ovaries intact. He told me my uterus was probably stuck to my bowels and the scar tissue needed to be removed. At twenty-nine years old, I was young and needed the ovaries to keep providing the necessary hormones for my body.

The Gynecologist was able to perform the surgery and followed his incision from a previous c-section scar so as to not mark up my body any more than absolutely necessary. He informed me after he was finished and I woke up in recovery, that he was unable to save my ovaries. Both had needed to be removed and were much too damaged by the scar tissue to try to salvage. He set me up on a regimen of prescription estrogen and would see me in six weeks for my check up. The hospital stay was a fairly short one. I had felt sooo much better after this surgery. I was free of that relentless pain! I am a firm believer in the fact that if you have finished bearing all the children you wish to have, and as a woman you are having severe problems… have it taken out!

I went to the office for my six week check up for the doctor to examine me. I had felt great and wanted to be released from any restrictions and go on with my life. He had explained that during the surgery where he had to take everything out, he had to form a sock so that I would be able to have sexual intercourse. The sock had not closed at the top and we needed to have another procedure. This time he was able to go in vaginally and fix, or darn the sock. This I must say was a very easy procedure as a patient to have gone through. I was out of the hospital the next day, and my husband and I had to wait another six weeks before we could engage in sexual relations.

CHAPTER 16

My Crohn's was under control with my smoke and the infusions of Remicade, and life was beginning to get back on track. Things were going well and this went on for the better part of a year, until one morning I woke up and stepped into the shower, I had sneezed in the shower and blew my nose, washing everything away. As I did this it felt like I had threw my back out. It hurt pretty badly, but didn't think much of it. This happened first thing in the morning around six o'clock. By the time seven rolled around the pain worsened and it was getting very difficult to breath. I frantically called around to different Chiropractors in my area, needing an emergency appointment. At eight o'clock I had finally reached one. The Chiropractor had asked me if I had ever had a lung collapse before. Of course I told him no. He was sure this is what it sounded like to him and urged me to go into the emergency room as soon as possible.

I got off the phone with him and drove myself to the local E-R. Precious time had passed and my breaths were harder and harder to intake. I remember looking at the nurse and asking to please knock me out before putting in the chest tube. She smiled very caringly and gave me a shot to save me from the pain. I woke up once again in one of the rooms of the hospital with my husband by my side. My surgeon was the one who had done the procedure and told me I had, had a blister or bleb on my lung that had burst. I stayed in the hospital for two weeks recovering. During this time my husband and I were trying to find answers as to why or how this had happened. The surgeon had no answers and we went home to search on the internet ourselves. We came home to the conclusion that the Remicade had weakened the tissue in the lung and had caused the bleb.

Only one week after being home from surgery did we need to go in for another infusion. We had explained our theory to my Gastroenterologist and he did not agree. He convinced us to go ahead and continue with the Remicade. Just after this infusion, feeling horrible and being in bed for several days, I was able to emerge and start to clean my house and perform everyday duties. At the end of the week… it happened again, only this time it was even harder to breathe than before, making it very difficult to even speak. I remember sitting on the couch trying not to move so that I could breath and calling my mother on the phone. I had asked her to pick me up to take me to the Emergency Room. I knew that this time I was not able to drive myself. She suggested I get a brown paper bag and breathe into it until she arrived. My three year old was glued to Dora the Explorer as I asked him to retrieve a brown bag from the kitchen. It was no use… Dora took precedence and I pretended that I was fine so that I wouldn't alarm him in any way.

I was unable to move from the couch and that impending doom washed over me once again. My mom arrived and she grabbed my three year old and we all got into the car. I remember telling her to drive faster, and if she didn't hurry that I was going to die in the car. Of course we hit every single red light on the way; I was yelling (as best as I could) "Run it! Just run the lights!" She was too scared and we waited at each one. She stopped at the doors of the emergency room when we arrived and I got out as she parked the car, I made it in the doors and collapsed on the floor. Hospital staff ran at me immediately and carried me off for another emergency surgery.

This time I woke up in the Intensive Care Unit for the first time ever. This was a little awkward, only because most of the folks working there had once had a job at the bar I had managed for so long. This was their full time professions, and they all took wonderful care of me. My surgeon had come in to tell me that they think they have fixed the problem for good. He explained that they had to go in this time and sew the blister up along with putting a fine powder or talc on the wound.

The recovery was very hard. I was worried; I was so weak, that I can't even explain. This time I was in the hospital for almost three weeks. One night I woke up from a dead sleep with hiccups. I pushed the call button and could only get out the words: "I need a knife!" When I was finally able to catch my breath I finished off with "Or a spoon, or a fork!" Staff came rushing in very confused. Only one male nurse knew exactly why I was yelling for a knife. He handed me the metal butter knife and a tall glass of water, I dropped the knife in the glass, then put the other end on my temple, and drank away. The hiccups from Hell had finally ceased. I couldn't imagine having a patient scream out for a knife in the middle of the night, I'm not so sure if I didn't know that was a remedy for hiccups that I would have given into that kind of strange request. We all laughed hysterically and the rest of the staff learned a new remedy for the common hiccup.

CHAPTER 17

After returning home, my husband and I decided to stop the Remicade. We had asked the Gastroenterologist at the next appointment for something else... *anything* else. He recommended a drug called Humera. I had to go and take a class on how to give myself a shot in the stomach, because I was to do this every other week... again for the rest of my life.

After a few months, I was not feeling any better. In fact I was able to feel my body literally deteriorate. By this time I had started to get rheumatoid arthritis and my joints would swell painfully. My knees swelled up so much that I needed the use of a cane to walk. My fingers had started to become nasty and deformed. My Crohn's had come back full force, and finding any kind of cannabis was almost impossible. I was no longer able to work, and my husband's employer had cut hours to the point where we could not afford to take the trips needed to see the Gastroenterologist.

Depression was starting to take hold as money was tight. I was forced to stop the bi-weekly shot. Pain was never ending, and my life was seemed to be coming to an end. I had become bedridden and felt that my family would be better off if I was gone. I thought that the life insurance would allow my family much needed financial relief, and I just wanted God to let me come home.

CHAPTER 18

Oil Progress

I have watched "Run from the Cure," the movie made by a man named Rick Simpson, who resides in Canada. This man is a hero to many, and I am no exception. I have watched the movie many, many times. Each time I have watched it, my eyes have wept with sadness, joy, and hope, all at one sitting. Once you see the movie, you will understand. You can watch it any time for free on the internet. Go to pheonixtears.ca follow the link on the left and enjoy! Canada claims to be free, just as we claim to be free here in America. Oh how I wish we were all *truly* free. I am unable to grow a plant in my yard that would allow me to heal myself. It is such a simple thing if you think about it.

I have actually tried almost every drug on the market for my disease, but only to find the simplest plant can alleviate my symptoms and pain better that any prescription pain medication ever could.

My husband and I had decided to purchase a cheap vaporizer (from cheapvaporizer.com), old school with a globe. Our own self-education was our means, the little thing is supposed to give more of a percentage of medication than any other form of inhalation. I was upset at first, it had taken me quite a while to learn how to work it. After inhaling the vapor, it was not alleviating my symptoms as well as smoking the cannabis. I was heartbroken and put it away.

After just a short while, I had gotten a hold of the harshest, worst-tasting weed that I had ever had in my life. I couldn't smoke it at all, the seed oil was so strong that vomiting was imminent. With no other options, I decided to pull out the vaporizer once again. My husband had noticed the beads of tar accumulating at the top of the glass when he came into the room to check on me. I had been reading a book, hiding in my room in the basement, and had lost track of time. We both thought of the movie right away! My finger could not reach as far as I desperately wanted it to reach to get as much of this stuff as I could. The taste is like no other I can describe. It has none of the familiar tastes associated with that particular plant at all. It is just a thick green or grassy taste—and not hard to get used to.

***

April 6, 2009

After a week and a half of using this method and using a small spatula to retrieve the smallest amount of oil, I have started to notice remarkable differences! I am proud to say that the first thing I noticed was that after two different lung surgeries (on the same lung) last year, I had severe nerve damage in my right breast. The breast felt as if I had an ugly case of mastitis. It took a long time after the surgery to convince me that they actually did not have problems during the procedure. I accused the doctors of dropping machinery on my chest. I even asked if there were problems as to where one of them would have gotten on my chest and dug their knee in my breast during some emergency unbeknownst to me. Needless to say, it was very painful. The pain slowly decreased in severity over the months but had never gone away—until now!

For the first time, I was finally able to feel joy and not wince in pain when my husband brushed his hand against my poor little excuse of a breast. Pure and simple blissful pleasures one tends to take far too much for granted. Throughout the first several days of trying this oil, the pain in my stomach had really not improved. The pain had actually gotten worse. My husband asked me if I thought it was a good pain or bad pain. I thought about it and decided that it might be good pain and to just deal with it.

I woke up this morning and pooped, and pooped, and pooped! When I thought I was done, I pooped some more! (Yes, that is a good thing!) Walking over to wash my hands, I felt my bowel fall away from high on my abdominal wall—on the highest point of where I have my abdominal scar from previous surgeries. The scar starts at the highest point at the bottom of my sternum and ends at the lowest point at my pelvis in a vertical fashion. As soon as I felt it drop away, I felt such relief! A great pressure was lifted! Not long after, I was droppin' a deuce once again! LOL!

I feel so good today that I felt as if I should write it all down and share my progress. I hope to cure myself completely and write a paper. Maybe send one to each one of the many doctors that I have come in contact over the years. Find a way to make this public at a future date and spread the news like a hot viral pancake. I want to scream my progress from the mountaintops and help Mr. Rick Simpson spread the word. However, since I am not completely healed, I am thinking about postponing until I am completely cured. I will not be able to put a good strong effort into it and fight on a political scale if I come out too soon. My fear is not speaking out soon enough! We will see how fast this stuff can work!

I am able to get only small amounts of the oil—much less than recommended in the movie. I am sure it will take a little more than three months to get completely cured. I am on the right track, this time the world better look out—nothing can stop me once I am healthy again! I will finally be able to accomplish the little things most others take for granted. I will be able to play and wrestle and roll on the floor with my family! I will be able to take walks! I will be able to attend each and every school function my children have! I will be able to spend an entire day out and about town—not having to take a break or worry about not completing the errands that need to get done! I will be able to have a clean house—every day! I will be able to cook meals for my family—every day! I will be able to enjoy my life and I will be free of these chains of pain that have been holding me hostage for so many years! I will once again laugh, dance, and be free! I will be able to walk down the street with my head held high, knowing that I receive pity from no one! Free! Free of pain, free of depression, the basic freedom to enjoy life once again! Never am I to take a breath of air, or the smell of a flower, or the sound of the wind, for granted—ever again!

CHAPTER 19

April 8, 2009

Yesterday I woke up feeling great again, but the stomach pain was much worse, just as it is today. I did have a bit of a scare yesterday. I think this stuff is working from the top of my body, down. Healing my breast and then the scar tissue on the back of my lung, from a blister or bleb that had popped on my lung, causing it to collapse twice. In order to fix this problem, the surgeon closed up the bleb and put a powder or talc of sand on the wound to cause friction against my ribs and cause a thick, strong growth of scar tissue so that it would not collapse again. I have always felt it pull a little on each breath, and now that it has gone, I no longer feel the pull of my ribs when I exhale. I had not even noticed that it was bothersome until it was gone—wow! I think I am going to continue to be amazed at how this stuff works.

I now have pain in my lower right abdomen. As I was having another glorious bowel movement, it felt like the bowel pulled away from the wall of my skin about an inch above my pelvis on the left side. As it pulled away, it felt as if it may have looped or gotten hung up on an organ and pulled it down. It didn't tickle much. That pain is finally gone today. Now it feels as if it may be working on my right abdomen and my main vertical scar in the middle of my tummy.

I do feel very energetic this morning, but we will see how the day plays out. I was also energetic yesterday morning to begin the day, but I couldn't find the energy to do much. It must be the cloudy weather. Bowel movements are much different, much harder, and more substantial than I have been used to in years. I am making much smoother deposits than I am used to. It has been too long for me to have had a semi-comfortable bowel movement. Think about that, just a minute ... Since 2002, my stools have been frequent, loose, and painful with as many as fifty trips to pay homage to my ungrateful porcelain god—every day. That would always determine, for me, what a good or bad day was by the amount of time I spent sitting and wasting away donating gifts to the porcelain god. Maybe now the big white porcelain god can't take anymore and I will be free from his curse! LOL!

The oil has yet to affect my arthritis, but hey, it has only been two weeks—if that—on this stuff. Miracles are happening! I must just stay patient—this will work and everything will work out! My biggest fear is that after I look back at my life as a healthy old woman, will these many years be just a blur as they feel now? Will I always be humble and grateful for this experience? I never want to forget the hardships that our family has had to face. I never want to forget the feeling when you know death is coming, eminent, looming. I want to be grateful for being sick. I would have never had my current education or knowledge of so many different aspects of life. I would have never taken the time or had the opportunity to sit still long enough to learn it. I am trying to be very grateful now. Now—more than ever—I am slowly being cured. I can feel it and believe it with every core of my being. The depths of my soul make me know that I am on the right track!

With new health, new knowledge, and a brand-new outlook on life, I will accomplish many things. I really hope to make a footprint in the system. Things are corrupt, and it saddens my heart to think that my family is not free. Realizing that we have not really been free for many generations makes me want, need, and hunger to make a difference.

Wish me luck!

CHAPTER 20

April 14, 2009

Wow! What a week it has been! My kitchen, living room, and bathroom have been clean for three days in a row! My laundry is up to par, and I have been doing very well! I am still a little slow at getting things done, but I'm coming around! Sunday was Easter—other than the weather affecting my arthritis, it was a great family day. My Crohn's even felt safe enough to cheat with a bit of a chocolate bunny! I did feel very tired all day Monday—I'm not sure if it was from the sweets or the weather.

I have been starting the day with my entocort (steroids). I want to finish the bottle off—just in case. I also take an herbal estrogen, because not having a uterus is a wonderful thing! I take a probiotic with fifty billion live flora for my tummy. I top off the pills with a B-17 vitamin, and that's when I take my oil. Throughout the day, I vaporize three to four "bowls," retrieving the gold with a spatula. So far, that has been doing fine. I want to point out another weird body-healing factoid. About eight months ago, I came down with a severe sinus infection. As a result of the infection, I got a NASTY pimple on my cheek. I have been battling this stupid little bastard forever! I started to just put a dab of the oil on it—it has been four days, and the improvement is amazing! I was very scared that it was going to leave an ugly scar on my face, but this oil is truly a miracle! It's almost gone! It really is the little things in life that make you happy.

My husband seems to be worried that I may be healing a little too fast. He thinks it may not be good because the concentrated THC kills abnormal cells and helps regenerate new healthy ones—supposedly without harming your body in any way. With other research we had found vitamin B-17. This vitamin essentially does the same thing. The problem with B-17 is that theoretically the B-17 produces natural cyanide produced by your own body, and that cyanide is what kills the abnormal cells. Theoretically, if you take too much, the cyanide may over-act, killing healthy cells as well. (This is no different from any form of radiation treatment, by the way). This defeats the purpose of trying to heal. Healing too fast may lead to further cell damage.

My personal thoughts however are much different. I don't know that I am getting enough of the stuff? I really do think it may take me longer with the amount I am able to retrieve at this point. I could heal so much faster! I am so close that I can taste it, and I want it more and more! Ahhhh! Life, breath, and the most precious of all: energy. Energy is so precious! When you have energy, you tend to be happy, energetic, and ready to take on whatever task that lays ahead! My energy level has skyrocketed! I am still taking it slow, but wow! I can't believe that just a month ago, I was lying in my bed in a ball of pain, waiting to die, or cry myself to sleep—I didn't care which came first. We have insurance, but with things the way they are, we just could not afford it. My thoughts at the time were that at least I would no longer be a burden on my friends or family, and a huge financial burden would be lifted on my husband. When the pain just won't let up and won't go away for days, depression is a horrible thing. If you fall too deep, it gets harder to climb out of that hole. I knew at the time that I was dying—your body knows and you feel impending doom at the core of your soul. You start to feel at peace with it. You know that your body is giving out, and you feel as if there is nothing left to do but wait for the calm and wait for the peace. I was almost ready to welcome it completely.

I have noticed on days when the sun shines, my energy—no matter how small of an improvement—improves. My husband also has done some research on orgone energy. I am now starting to truly believe in it! It can be hard to wrap your brain around, but let's see if I can describe it in a way that gives it justice. Orgone energy is the energy of the earth and the natural energy of the sun. All things have their own energy, Trees, grass, and flowers all give off frequencies of energy. The orgone energy is floating everywhere. On a sunny, clear day, look into the sky and notice the white floating, bouncing particles in the air. It is not dust—it is theoretically orgone energy. There are ways to harness it. Many scientists and doctors have studied and written books on the subject, but it is usually shrugged off by their colleagues. It is well worth the research. They were able to contain the orgone and cure cancers and other ailments. They had also found that too much exposure was very harmful.

Always keep an open mind when you are looking for truth. If you remember that philosophy is just opinion, then you will find a world full of knowledge for you to fork and sift through. Things slowly start to fit together like a big puzzle in your brain. You start to take that knowledge and link it to everything you know, and things start to "click." I keep having these moments where things will click in my mind and I will look at the entire world in a new way. On certain things, it will just mess me up for a week or two, so I can ponder on it, wrap my head around it, and make sense of the world. First falling deeper in depression and then waking up to help to inform others of simple truths of life. The tough thing to get used to is that the more you learn, the more questions you have. All answers lead to more questions, so the personal fire to retrieve knowledge can flame, smolder, and smoke. For me, it always flames right back up again to restart the cycle once more.

The sun is up, and it should be warm today. I make small goals each day. I have been able to keep up on my house and achieve those small goals. Now to step it up, this week I hope to clean my horrendous office and basement, which have both become catchalls for crap around the house. One day, I will have an immaculate house with nice things, but not until the boys get older. Ahhh, boys—running, jumping, screaming, muddy—and the smell of wet dog. I love every bit of it!

CHAPTER 21

April 25, 2009

It's a very early Saturday morning. I still have not been sleeping well, but I have had a ton of energy most of the week! My house is still clean! I have dropped my entocort down to one pill on this week. I felt good enough that when a friend of mine asked me to show her different exercises for different muscles, I ended up giving her one hell of a workout, doing it myself in the process! I felt great the rest of the day! It was not until that night that I felt the effects of the workout. That on top of all the housework I've been up to as well as cleaning both vehicles.

My Crohny poop came back Thursday night. I have been attributing it to the amount of sit-ups that I had done. I have been feeling scar tissue rip, break, and fall away from my bowels. When I feel it in my bowels, it is as if something suddenly releases and my bowels will fall and relax. I tend to have a bowel movement shortly after. The BM produced is almost always pasty like peanut butter and is painful to produce. I rough through it because I know in my soul that it is the healing process and is going to take some time. I woke up this morning at five and have pooped more times than I can count. It is now only seven and my rectum is highly inflamed and burning with a little bleeding. My bowels this morning are on fire and I am fixing to try the oil on a generic brand of hemorrhoidal suppository. I am hoping that direct contact will eventually help my current situation. At this point, I can smoke myself stupid and it will not help the pain.

CHAPTER 22

April 27, 2009

Do *not* try the oil on a suppository while rectal bleeding is occurring!!! I am pretty sure that it works just fine—but it burns like *hellfire*! Now, with that said, I still tried it again. When the rectum is not bleeding, the oil is fine. There is a warming sensation, but it seems to me that it kicks it in high gear. I have pretty much been out for the count for the last two days. Saturday I was in so much pain, during the process of working out, I think it was bowel releasing from muscle on both sides of the muscle, on the front between my skin and abdominal muscle, also on the back end, the bowel had become attached to my muscle and had ripped away. This is really not surprising considering a large amount of my surgeries consisted of removal of vast amounts of scar tissue causing organs to stick together. This was the main reason that I had a complete hysterectomy at the age of twenty-nine. Don't get me wrong, I embrace it. Anything that makes you constantly bleed for five to seven days and doesn't kill you is evil in my book!

Back to the topic, I have been trying to heal the sores on my bowel because of it. I had to take two pain pills for the pain to get some relief. I'm not sure, but I also think that my body was just so exhausted from pooping so much that I needed the sleep. So, I stayed in bed from Saturday afternoon all the way through to Monday morning. Sunday my bowels felt like I had just had surgery, so very raw. I had gotten chills and was very cold all day. I had taken breaks to eat, smoke, take medication, and of course poop some more. Over the last several days, my bowel movements have been frequent, painful, and pasty. For the first time in I don't know how long—even though I have been so ill that it had made me stay in bed—I know I am healing. I have a certain sense of calm about me. I think that I had felt so good, I allowed myself to exercise much too quickly and far too early in the healing process. On the other hand, I think it needed to be done—I can stretch back farther and reach my hands higher than I had before. After the exercises, I stretched my stomach to intentionally rip things away. I have done it in the past, but never with such results! I can take the pain, I know I am getting better. I had just not expected to rip away so much and I believe this is the first time I have felt it rip away from muscle.

I have been taking the oil as I need it. I went through quite a bit this weekend and, this morning, I felt comfortable enough to try a suppository again. This would be the third or fourth time I have done this. Each time, I feel much better within the hour. Today is a new day and I feel a lot better. I can't wait to see how much housework I can catch up on! I've noticed that the oil has a side effect that I have not seen any other information on. It sticks to your teeth a bit and looks as if it is staining them, but it is not. I try to only dry brush it off if I am going somewhere or expecting company. That way I can massage it into my gums. I have a tooth in the back that the filling has come off of and I brush the oil on. Pain that I did not realize I had was gone! Not only that, but I do believe my teeth are getting stronger and whiter. I'm not sure if that has to do with oil—but I bet it does!

CHAPTER 23

April 30, 2009

Crap! Now I am out of medication (weed). I have started to feel pretty darn good, and I hope that I can get more meds soon. So far, I must say that it feels as if this oil has taken three to five years off my disease! Maybe it won't take as long as I once thought to get better!

CHAPTER 24

May 8, 2009

I am still out of medication. Before I started today, I looked at my last entry. It has only been a smidgen over a week since I have been able to have oil, but it feels like it's been two. Like any other poor and conservative smoker, I resulted to smoking roaches. When you roll a cigarette, you are only able to smoke it so far before it burns your fingers. If you are resourceful, you save the ends, called roaches, to break up and make new joints. Smoking roaches are *nasty*! The taste is vile and the smell is nauseating, but it will get the job done when you are desperate. Well, I was desperate. I decided to try to vaporize the roaches, I didn't want to stop the oil process.

Warning   **Warning**   **Warning**

Okay—do not vaporize the oil and eat it from a roach! Even though there is a very slight resemblance to the good stuff, I would have had a better taste in my mouth if I had licked an ashtray full of Winstons. At that point, I decided, well if I can't eat it that way—yup! I just ate it from the other end. I was able to do this for two days. I guess that, even if you eat it at the other end, it doesn't stop the nasty ashy taste from arriving on your tongue. The realization of having that nastiness stain the vaporizer made me stop.

I was able to get only a small amount of medication, which has meant that I have been smoking it and postponing the oil. Over the week, I have slowly regressed. My blockage is trying to come back at the top of my belly, and my Crohny poop missed me. I must muster through. I will not go back to how I once felt. I'm a million miles away from where I was before I started the oil. I think I am just getting impatient. I feel as if someone dangled this great life full of hopes and dreams in front of me and then just snatched away the rug from under me—only for that person to sit, head tilted back, and laugh. Holding on at this point, waiting and waiting, is like being in purgatory.

CHAPTER 25

May 16, 2009

My husband was finally able to find some medication. He came downstairs Mother's Day evening at 11:30. I had spent those last few days in bed, I hide when I'm not feeling well. I don't like to have my children see me when I'm in that much pain. There are times when I cry out uncontrollably or when I burst into tears because the pain is so overpowering. He was my knight in shining armor that night—I was finally *free!* It had taken around three days to get back to feeling really well. I am still feeling scar tissue pull away, this time around, however, is not nearly as painful. It feels as if most of the scar tissue has fallen away from my abdominal cavity—save for a small area at the top of my vertical scar on the top of my belly. In addition, I still feel pulling in my back on my lower right ribs. For the most part, it's as if my bowels have fallen and relaxed into a hard mass.

I have felt something similar in the past. When my youngest son was born prematurely with an emergency c-section, I was awake when the anesthesia failed. I felt the knife cut into my skin, and it felt as if a hot piece of metal was burning me open. I felt the skin open and the doctors shove a piece of metal in to keep the skin stretched open. I could feel the corner of the cut stretch with fire as I felt hands touch the outside of my uterus. I had always thought that organs were smooth and silky—not the uterus full of water and child. It feels flaky with tags of skin hanging off, and I could feel each one as the hands of the physician measured my womb to find the safest and quickest way to get the child out. I only felt pressure on the womb when the water broke, but there was no pain when the skin of it opened up. I was able to lay eyes on him before they carted him away and the anesthesiologist knocked me out to sew me back up. I awoke in the hospital bed, and it was found that I had some internal bleeding. I then had my first blood transfusion, from losing two pints of blood. My obstetrician had decided that I could use the iron from the blood loss that had just accumulated in my gut—making it swell—and allowed my body to naturally absorb the blood back into my system. A large mass formed in my abdomen. The smaller it got, the harder it got—until it was finally gone. The feeling of my bowels now feels very similar to the large, hardening blood clot that once inhibited my abdomen before it started to get smaller.

My energy level is back up, I have now had a full week's worth of the oil and only have enough for one more week. It seems so absolutely stupid to me that anyone would look at me as a criminal. I am only trying to get back to any kind of normalcy for me and my family. I have found my "Fountain of Youth." I have found, for the first time *ever*, the one and only thing that makes me feel remotely how I did before I was cursed with this disease. I don't feel high; I feel **alive!** I can now think much more clearly because I no longer think about the pain. I never fully realized that your brain cannot focus or function on other things when you're in pain. Pain has stolen years away from me. Pain has taken so much—energy, life, happiness, and health.

If a single plant on this earth could cure anything and could be readily available to anyone who had access to some dirt, then the pharmaceutical companies would have no way to make money off of the public. How can you patent a plant? That of course would have an effect on major industries—insurance companies, hospitals, pharmacists and the cool drugs they make with the awesome TV ads; the list goes on.

If people only knew what a crock it all was! It was a big step for me, taking my life in my own hands and no longer believing that anyone else other than me has had my best interests at heart. It is not all the physician's fault. He has had years and years of medical school teaching him that these new pharmaceuticals are the way to go. He is brainwashed into thinking that—even though a high percentage of people they prescribe chemotherapy die. They believe that the ones that are strong enough to survive are just in their survival—and the ones who lost that battle, well, it was just meant to be. These poor men pay high dollar for their education, feeling that they are not significant enough to second-guess the system. The system must know best—right? When folks no longer second-guess, when they only just "take their word for it," they end up being followers of a false truth. Statistically, there are always more followers than leaders—especially in the medical field. It's all politics, baby, and all about the almighty dollar.

Finding this truth out for myself is the best thing that has ever happened to me! I feel like I have won the lottery! I won a new chance on life. The difference here is that I can now help others win as well! I can't stop thinking of those who have needlessly lost their lives under the care of the medical system. I can't stress enough that you must take your life into your own hands. I hope that writing this journal will open the minds of many so that they can truly see their own miracles come true!

Rick Simpson has opened the door and is paving the way as an example of how humanity treats each other. This man is my hero and I hope to follow in his footsteps by spreading the message of truth and exposing the medical community for what they truly are—thieves.

I have been outside most of this week; the sun has been out, and the weather has been in the upper seventies. I planted some vegetables and flowers, spending a good four hours at one stretch in the sun. I have red hair and very fair skin. I normally will burn in the sun within the fifteen minutes it takes to mow the front lawn. Anyhow, I needed to plant these things, I had waited too long and I was regretting the evening knowing my body was surely as red as a beet. My skin was sore and warm, but nothing more. I woke the next day, no tan, no burn—nothing!

Never in my entire life has this ever happened to me! I have always burned in the sun. I have had blisters rise on my skin by almost two inches! Ah, man, are they painful! A bad burn will make your body feel like you had the flu for a good seventy-two hours. That is exactly what I had expected —but nothing!

This oil is truly amazing! This morning, as I was retrieving my oil from my globe, the rubber seal went a bit off kilter, so I stupidly went to grab and pull it straight. The metal gets very hot. The knuckle of my thumb touched the metal and I could actually hear the skin singe and smell it burn like burnt hair. I looked at my thumb and a blister had formed and risen considerably. With fresh oil on my trusty spatula, I dabbed some on and bandaged it up. Immediately, the burning was gone. Within minutes the blister was gone, and two hours later, you can't even tell that it's there! I am able to actually rub my finger on it and it looks as if the scar is a week old!

I am just flabbergasted by the potential this stuff has! If gold ever had a flavor, the oil is it! I only hope and pray that I can get this message out and not harm myself or my family in the process. My husband said something that keeps sticking with me—"In each life-changing situation, it is always better to be safe and cautious."

On a side note: I had completed the entocort, of course just in time to run out of my hemp along with my B-17, I am proud to say that along with my oil, I now only take a natural estrogen supplement, one calcium pill, and a probiotic. The probiotic will be gone in three days, and we don't have the money for another fifty-dollar bottle, so we will see! I have no doubt in my mind that as long as I have the oil, I will be just fine!

CHAPTER 26

May 31, 2009

Wow! What can I say? I now only take an herbal estrogen once a day along with my oil and smoke. It has been a bit of a struggle lately to get any amount of medication, I've only been able to get quarter- or eighth-bags. This has forced me to cut back on the oil. I think I feel as if I have plateaued for a while—keeping just enough in my system, then running out for a day or two and doing the process over. Not able to get over a much-needed hump. I say that and then I think to myself that I am being ungrateful because I still have accomplished sooo much in these past weeks! We took a last-minute family trip that we really could not afford, but we went to the beautiful mountains. A full three days of busy sightseeing, visiting, and making new friends. From the minute we left, we have all felt homesick! I felt pretty good, I had gotten tired at times, but I was smart and got the rest I needed.

The entire trip was fantastic! I can't stop thinking about stepping out on the porch first thing in the morning on the top of the mountain—actually in the clouds with the sun still shining above. The energy is so great in the air that it really does feel as if you are closer to the heavens. It leaves that rare warmth, peace, and love that fills up your heart and makes you want to fall to your knees and cry like an infant child in pure happiness—allowing the heavens complete access to your mind, body, and soul. I can't wait to get back! Since we have no experience in the mountains I was worried at first. It was rainy and cold the first night we arrived; we even had to drive through thick hail up the mountain.

The boys and men were outside most of the evening. When my five-year-old came in to take a bath, he cried because his feet hurt. I figured that he had a small case of frostbite and rubbed his feet. He woke up in the middle of the night crying in pain, so I rubbed some more and he would go back to sleep. He was fine the next day. We had a spare pair of dry shoes, and he was off to play and never complained. That night, it was storming again and we were about to eat supper when he started to cry again, uncontrollably, pleading for us to help him. That kind of cry tears at your heart. I have never had any experience with frostbite, but the top of his foot—from his toes to the middle—was cherry red and hot to the touch. It also spread to the entire bottom of his feet. The only thing that alleviated his pain was constant massage on both feet at once. I was not able to stop for a moment. We all felt helpless—on top of a mountain during a bad storm—we had nowhere to go. I thought of the oil! It seemed to take forever to make, but I put just a dab on my finger and mixed it with lotion and rubbed it on. He was relieved immediately! The foot was still red, but we put on socks and finished supper. I checked first thing in the morning and both his feet were perfectly colored and no sign at all of frostbite!

CHAPTER 27

June 4, 2009

I have been feeling well. I've been very picky with my diet as late and have been trying more raw food. The oil I have been taking has allowed my body to process it. I am slowly introducing sprouts, sunflower seeds, cabbage, cauliflower, carrots, broccoli, and dry ramen noodles in a salad with some zesty Italian dressing. I have been finding that introducing this does give me pain in my stomach, but at the same time, it gives me energy and nutrition I do not normally feel after a meal. I have so far been able to have it pass through—I think it may be helping other food pass through too! The blockage or knot at the top of my stomach is still present.

I do however feel that the oil is starting to work its magic once again. The pain tells me that it is working, so I hope to have relief soon. The scar tissue is still constantly coming loose. I had a large amount rip off of my uterine sock. I felt the bowel come away between my skin and my c-section scar and the uterine sock. It just ripped away and fell to join the lump of bowel in the middle—all during fantastic intercourse with my husband. Believe it or not, making love or having sex has on more than one occasion saved me. If my husband and I do not participate with one another for more than one week, my bowels get worse with scar tissue. For years, I have needed him just as much as he has needed me. Having a healthy sex life—even when you are sick—is a dire need. We have toughed it out and have had to wait months, but it is always worth it in the end. He has always joked that his "protein" can fix anything. I am constantly rolling my eyes with a smile. The fact is that after frolicking in the bedroom with my husband, I have noticed I end up having energy. There might just be a little truth in his "protein" idea. In the evening, just lying in bed wanting nothing more than to please your partner and your partner wants the same for you. Spending yourself completely of energy and falling to sleep in bliss. Waking in the morning on those days after a long hard sleep is simply the best! It helps to heal not only your body, but also your soul—making you and your companion come closer together and fall deeper in love during each encounter. My advice is to have sex—lots of it if you're able. Even when you are very sick, allowing your partner to pleasure you will help him or her to know that you feel better—if just for a short while. It is so gratifying for your partner to know that he was able to make you feel better in any way—and the benefits to your sick body are numerable. Now that I have endorsed erotic pleasures for the sick, let me get back to the oil and other benefits besides the libido … apparently.

I mentioned that the oil helped an infected tooth that the filling had come off of. I remember watching a YouTube video of a newscast in Germany. The news was of a German concrete maker who put cannabis into her mixture. The mixture was stronger, lighter, and used less material. I used that philosophy to mix a small amount of my oil with an over-the-counter tooth filler. I rubbed it into a ball and mixed it together. I packed it into the tooth the best that I could. I used wax paper and gum to finish the job. I just so happened to have an ionic whitening system, so I used the blue light from the mouthpiece, hoping it would be like the one the dentist uses in his office—resulting in a hardening of the cap. It has been four weeks and the cap is still in place—no problems and no more pain!

I would like to pull my dental records sometime soon. These will show severe cavities along the base of my gum line. Crohn's disease affects the entire digestive system, and your mouth and teeth are no exception. The cavities were formed from brushing and causing ruts and grooves along the gum line. I'm not sure how many cavities I once had, and I'm not sure how bad my gingivitis was either. I have been rubbing the oil on my cavities along my gum line that were completely black in color to start. They went from black to gray to brown, and now they are starting to whiten. The teeth themselves are healing from the inside out! Now I only have a few black spots, and the teeth are grayish-yellow turning to a pale white.

Those claims are impossible in the medical community! You are not supposed to be able to heal cavities! You are not supposed to heal or get rid of scar tissue or Crohn's disease either! These claims will be laughed at and scoffed at by the medical community. The medical community as a whole may collapse—only needing medical personnel to fix us up during trauma or an accident. Hell, if during that process, the oil was used, I'm sure downtime and recovery will be dramatic and fast.

I'm sorry—ridicule me if you wish for saying what I'm about to say, but so be it. I do not care one iota if every medical specialist in the country went out of business. The time for change is now! Let them all go out of business and join the rest of us in these hard financial times. The amount of money that went from my household was enormous; it is all about the money and your life no longer matters when you are just a statistic on the page. Every single American in this country has been railroaded into the idealology that we must spend a large portion of our income for healthcare and then pay for healthcare for those that can't afford it—only to be slowly killed off unknowingly by the medical community. Our government has known that concentrated THC oil can cure cancer and other ailments since 1974! That was three years before I was even born! I have lived in absolute hell for eight years. I had my life and youth stolen from me! For what? So that these professionals can stay in business? Do they think the country will collapse? For the greater good? My shiny white ass!!! I am risking so much by taking my life into my own hands, but if I am just one of many who join together and stand up and teach one another how to do this themselves, we can take back our freedom and the new world ahead will be a bright and hopeful one for mankind.

I am slowly teaching myself to garden and to cook from scratch. I am proud to say that I can now make the most delicious bread and rolls completely from scratch. It's a good thing, too—I don't know how many loaves of bread I had to put in the trash! I must continue to learn how to grow my own produce, and I intend to learn how to can and dehydrate things. I am trying to teach myself the basics in life that most busy folks don't have the time to learn. If I am to promote my idea of living off the grid, I need to practice what I preach.

I am finding the transition to be very gratifying on a grand scale. The simple thing of making something with your hands that is useful and pleasing for your family is so awesome. Having a child old enough to do the dishes afterword is priceless. ;.) As I transition into this new life and take my family along that path as well, I hope to find easy and inexpensive solutions to help anyone else who would like to join us. We can all do it!

CHAPTER 28

June 11, 2009

I have been feeling great! I still have plenty of energy—even though the last several days have been a little rough. With all the activity I have been doing, things are still coming loose. I went to the zoo with my mom and my kids. We walked the entire thing, and it took about three hours to do it! I never had to sit or take a break once! In fact, when we stopped by the monkey exhibit, I was the first one to see the monkey bars off to the side. Of course, the boys beat me to it, but I got on and successfully made it to the other side! I am so proud of myself! That is huge for me! My first baby steps! I still have a mountain to climb, but climb, I will! Later that same afternoon, I bravely got on my son's motorbike and took it out for a spin. First gear and wide fifty-foot turns were all I could handle, but that was good enough for me. It was also stupid on my part, as I did not have a helmet—bad mommy!

I have also been cleaning my house like a madwoman! I am, by nature, a deep cleaner. You would think that would not be a problem, but it is. I am not satisfied until something is completely clean, so I'm rarely satisfied. Being sick over the years and having no energy, I would end up spending the week trying to catch up on laundry, while only having the energy a couple of days a week—or sometimes month—to clean the house. Years of crap are all over the place. I have been playing catch-up like you would not believe. Before, I would finally get the kitchen clean and might get to one of my two bathrooms, but that was rare—and then I would be down from overworking myself for at least a week and sometimes two or more. When I mustered up all of my strength, I would do it all over again, creating a vicious cycle.

My poor family only got a meal two or three times a week—if they were lucky. The dishes could sit for days until I had the strength to tackle them. Now, it is completely different! I have been cooking every day and have been trying to do it all from scratch! Last night, I made pizza dough, and the boys thought it was delicious. I put too much cheese on it for me to handle and had some Raisin Bran.

I have been cleaning every day, and the boys are helping so much! I even rearranged my living room for the first time in five years! When my oldest was just a baby, I cleaned my whole house every day and rearranged my living room at least once a month! Over the years, I can now see as I look back how my energy was slowly sucked out by my disease.

My weight has maintained a steady 115–120 pounds for the last several months that I've been on the oil. After getting out of the shower, a couple of days ago, I stepped out and bent over to dry my hair and glanced at my sagging skin hanging down from my stomach. At one point, I think my body ballooned to 165 pounds back when I was drugged up on prednisone. I remember looking in the mirror and only being able to recognize my eyes looking back at me. The skin on my face would stretch and swell and felt as if I were in a costume or suit that I couldn't get out of. With the weight gone, I was staring at the skin sagging from my tummy, I noticed something strange. The skin from the right side of my scar hung low and you could flap it. LOL! The skin on the left of the scar was still in place. I grabbed what was still in place and wiggled and jiggled it. I have been stretching and moving, but I am still trying to get it loose days later. It is attached to the blockage that I still have high on my stomach.

I have also put the oil in some face cream and have been putting it on my face and stomach for weeks now. I can see a dramatic reduction in my wrinkles and, when I put it on my tummy, I'm just hoping to get more oil to the area. Just months ago, I was looking really bad—I had a boil on my face, and depression and sickness took its toll as deep lines of wrinkles on my forehead, between my eyes, my crow's feet, and deep lines around my mouth. I will be thirty-two years old in just a few days and went from looking like I was forty to looking like I'm in my twenties!

There are times now when I am in pain, but I can still get through it and not stop what I'm doing. I have not had to lie on the couch for weeks now! I may stop to sit or take a small break, but I get right back up for more. I feel as if I have so much to do. I feel rushed, and my life feels chaotic. I love that! I am one of those people that just functions better when more things are going on.

The more I have on my plate, the harder and more focused I can work. I have always found that having less work makes you lazy. Everyone is entitled to a lazy day once in a while, but if there is no work to do, the laziness will take over. The point is that the more that I have to do the happier and more productive I am. I am happiest working behind the bar—being so busy that you have no time to think about anything except the job at hand. Being in the "zone" and moving and spinning and working in sync with another person behind a small bar is so much fun for me! What is a better job than making people smile and have a good time? I miss it very much.

CHAPTER 29

June 26, 2009

This has just been the best! Last week was my birthday, and I can't remember the last one I spent out of the hospital. This one was *fantastic*! My husband started the week by taking our boys to Oklahoma to see their grandparents, he did this in one day. When he got some rest, we took a trip to Colorado and had a great time looking for employment and housing. After we got back, we went to Nebraska for our younger brother's wedding. Then, we came home again, only to leave two days later, back to Oklahoma to pick up our boys. I never travel. Until now, traveling was just not feasible. I was constantly nauseated, and I never knew when a bowel movement would creep up on me. On top of that, what little energy I did have was sucked away by traveling any substantial distance.

Although I am feeling fantastic, I have felt drained since coming home from so much travel. I have been trying to take a nap here and there to try to allow my body to rest. Yesterday I woke from an afternoon nap to find that Michael Jackson had died from a heart attack. I have been truly heartbroken. Anyone who knows me well has teased me about him being my childhood idol. Not so much for his music as what he stood for and opened my eyes to as a child. For me, Michael represented a true loving soul. His heart truly went out to others less fortunate, and he was one of the first in my opinion to bring forth the need to help those who really had it rough. His song "Man in the Mirror" is my absolute favorite of all time. I have never been able to sit through that song without singing with my heart and sobbing like a baby. Now—more than ever—I want to make a difference. I know that I can and will make the world a better place.

CHAPTER 30

July 6, 2009

I believe that before I got sick, I was not able to feel the things in my body as I do now. For me, the longer I was sick—each pain, twinge, or wrench that I had—made me more aware of my body, Such as where organs are located and how they feel within my own body. With each surgery I have ever had, I felt the different organs heal afterward, making me very aware of their presence. Since I had continually seen physicians over the years, I was very honest and would tell them what I felt was wrong when I was having pain. That is what you are supposed to do, right? My surgeon would tell me I shouldn't feel or know where things are. He said, "The body doesn't work like that—you can't feel your organs." I think by the way he talked down to me—as if I was two or was impaired to hear too fast—that he thought I was actually losing my mind! It was all in my head, right? **Absolutely *not*!** Please don't ever let another person second-guess what your body is telling you. **You**—and only **you**—know what is going on in there! However, I did make the mistake of letting that happen, and I would second-guess my own sanity. At the time, I really was such a naive person.

Now I am able to easily feel and know what things are generally doing in there. My bowels are not as hard as they used to be. I had a bout last week for three days in a row. I had hiccups and pain under my sternum. The scar tissue attached to my diaphragm was tugging at it and pulling it down. Stretching and sleeping helped it over a few days, along with my homemade lotion with the oil in it. I rubbed it all over my tummy. Other than that, I have been very active ... Still!

CHAPTER 31

July 10, 2009

I ran out of marijuana on the Fourth of July weekend. This time had not been nearly as bad as not having any oil. This time was much easier on me than the previous two times before. My Crohny poo had not returned once! Surprisingly, for five days I was without my green goodness and the first three went very well. I still had energy and was still cleaning the house and so forth. On the fourth day, I could feel my stomach try to tighten, and it was as if my scar tissue was waking up to take over once again. I still have that blockage up high on my abdomen and am now convinced more than ever that it's nothing more than scar tissue tightening around whatever it can find. I am starting to think that my struggle with Crohn's disease may be coming to a close. It also looks as if I may have a long battle yet to come to diminish the immense scar tissue plaguing my little body.

I've been having problems with hiccups for a couple of weeks now. I could feel scar tissue on my diaphragm pulling down toward my bowels. It hurt so badly the other day that I got worried for the first time. I have stopped stretching to take it a little easier on my body. Life has been good, and I am now focused on the bigger picture in all of this. I am slowly and discreetly spreading the word to try to save as many lives as I can. I am still learning and doing as much research on the subject of the oil and the plant—including the laws, regulations, and different state standards. In my state, if I was to get caught with any amount of marijuana, I would not be allowed to bring up my medical history as a defense. The state would lock up a loving mother and wife who is only struggling to live on a daily basis. I would be locked up and treated as a criminal thug, with no say in the matter whatsoever.

I am ready! I have decided that if that happens before I have a chance to move out of this godforsaken state, I will just have to show up to court before the judge and jury in a bikini! Anyone who had eyes would clearly see my massively mutilated body and the scars that the surgeons have left behind. A person's eyes can't be fooled! What would the world do then? My close and dear friends would picket outside to set me free! The media would be brought in to expose the system and show the cure to the world! Helping to spread a new health revolution where we don't need our government to hold our hands to comfort us as they pump poisons such as chemo into your body—even though they know it could kill you.

I am also feeling that I'm almost at the finish line! Each time I run out of oil or smoke, the finish line gets a little farther, but I never stray from the track. I know that it works, so I faithfully keep on pushing myself. I will finish and win this race! The difference I see in my family and myself seems absolutely amazing to me! My husband and children are so much happier now. The kids are not able to get away with things they once could, and even though they say they don't like it, it gives them structure, and they are all around much happier for it. With the oil, I no longer need any other medication other than herbal estrogen and vitamins. I can now fix any cut, burn, bite, or sickness of any kind on my own! Our family will only need to see a physician if severe trauma has occurred or physical harm is involved.

Things are going to start turning in our favor. I am healing and trying to find a way to help others. I have been waiting for years for this hell to end! Now that we have gone through such heartache and trauma, in our lives that we are going to see a huge turn in the road! Our future is bright and full of excitement! The daily, drastic changes in the world bring me to a subject I was unsure of how to write about until now. I'm not sure, but as of late, I have started to really believe in what happened to me. For so long, none of it made any sense, but now things are starting to happen in this world that are causing me to believe in the validity of it.

Early in 2007, I smoked some stuff that was very euphoric. I felt pretty good. It took my pain and nausea away immediately. I sat back in my chair and everything went white. It was very bright and warm—like white noise—but with a light that filled my head. I was flooded with information; my mind was flooded with images and information. It's the kind of knowledge that you receive from your inner-self. I can only compare it to a pregnant woman knowing whether her child will be a boy or a girl or a man walking down the street, sensing danger around the corner and finding it. It was knowledge that was given to me and I was just to know it.

I was blessed as a child to have a mother with an open mind. I was not forced to go to church. My mother encouraged me to look at many religions, and when I got old enough, I could decide for myself where I wanted to go to church. Growing up, I went to many different churches with friends. I have done my own research on religion. I came to the conclusion as a young teen that I did not like any organized religion. I believe in God, but not when half of a service for God is spent asking for money.

I believe that you find God in yourself. I read the Bible as stories told from the past. They are just stories told by men, explaining their history and experiences. The church—having their own itinerary—selected chosen books of the Bible and omitted others to manipulate populations. I believe that government and church are very similar. They both are interpreted to suit whatever point they are trying to make. The law is written to protect the "average man." However, the government has grown to interpret the Constitution as they see fit. The church is the same way only including certain books of the Bible and excluding others for fear of contradiction in what the church feels is better for the "average person", interpreting the Bible as they see fit.

I have always believed in God and prayer on a basic and core level. I claim no religion, and at this point writing about this vision I had … is the first time I have actually put it on paper, for great fear of folks claiming I may be a crazy loon! This vision that I had only lasted a few seconds, but there was so much information and knowledge given to me in pieces that none of it made any sense. This vision told me that I will become a huge public figure. That people will look at my husband and I as a true American family, because of our interracial status. That I will have many followers, and that folks will look at me more religiously than politically; That, I need to make sure that I am looked at as a political figure, not as any religious figure. At the time, it made no sense to me. I had never had any interest whatsoever in my entire life in being a political figure. I didn't understand politics at that time and have rarely met a politician that I cared too much for. My vision told me that I needed to be prepared because the public will push hard for me to run for office to speak up for the people.

The fact that anyone would look at me in any religious way has scared the crap out of me from day one of my vision—and it never made any sense. How can anyone look at me or follow me religiously when I have never claimed any religion? In fact, whenever I am asked about what religion I am, I have always joked and said that I practice "Shona-ism." I explain that I find my own way to pray and worship God but that I conform to no organized religion.

My husband, who was force-fed the Bible and its stories as a child, has just brought to my attention certain stories about Jesus that we had both forgotten. Jesus himself carried around this "holy anointed oil" that he used to heal and cure others and has been documented in the Bible as such. Also, at the end of his life, it has been said that the women who went into his crypt poured this anointed oil all over Jesus's body. That is when his body disappeared. Over time, religions all over the world have celebrated this miraculous time as Good Friday to Easter Sunday. With my own research, I find that there are many different versions of the stories of Jesus. For the most part, Jesus used an ointment that could have contained the oil. The one time the Bible does specify any kind of oil is just before the Last Supper and a woman from off the street comes in and pours an oil of some kind all over Jesus's head. His disciples were upset because the oil was worth very much money and could have been sold. In one story, Jesus explains that she was only trying to help and that a statue or monument should be made in her honor for what she had done. I have been trying to find anything on this woman and have so far been unsuccessful. I have been unable to find any ingredients of what we would think the oil is or what it was made of and have yet to find the ingredients of what was used in the ointment. My search will continue.

What if this oil made from the marijuana plant is the same oil that Jesus himself used?

The implications of that simple question are mindboggling.

The point is that this would now explain the religious factor in my vision, yet still doesn't put much together; leaving me to wonder whether or not I should risk speaking to a religious figure about my experience. I still have severe reservations about "coming out" with this vision.

Here is another reason; It was told to me that we all, as in humanity itself, need to become self-sufficient. That I needed to find a way to teach the public about off-the-grid living on a massive scale to make it easier for everyone for conversion. It was told to me that we need to do this because of a war that is going to plague this country and... the world for that matter. That, Governments will combine and turn our lives into a police state, controlling every aspect of the lives of everyday people all over the world. There will be the greatest civil unrest of all time. A revolution that will cross the globe will arise and I am to be a great part of that. Somewhere in that mess, I am supposed to lead the people, speak out against corruption and control, and help to rebuild a new world.

Do you see how crazy that sounds! It however makes my hands shake as I write this! The knowledge is overpowering. It's more like a truth that I must prepare my family, neighbors, friends, and community for—the world for that matter. I feel this constant urgency to speak out and to warn people of what is to come. I am just still unsure of how to explain myself and of how people will react when I try to explain that I'm not a crazy person that I did not ask for this. I'm just a normal person; I have never had this happen to me before. Also this experience is far too real to just shake off anymore. Things are happening, and I can't help but think that I must take this seriously and learn what I can before the shit hits the fan. I myself still have reservations and have a small part telling me that I'm crazy and that it was just the "Jesus Weed," and that I shouldn't even be putting any of this to ink. However, that part just keeps getting smaller and smaller as the days go by. That is why I need to write these things down.

I have been inspired by my vision to write several business plans. Immediately after my vision in 2007, I rewrote my original coffeehouse plan and turned it into a community-meeting place. The idea was to place a coffeehouse, an Italian restaurant, a pub, and an energy store on the same location placed in a circle with a central meeting area. Every self-sufficient building will have everything you need to do it yourself in your own home. My theory is that if you can have a waiter in a fancy restaurant tell you the name of the fish that you are eating, the part of the world where it was caught, and the name of the fisherman who caught it, then you can teach anyone to do the same when it comes to recycling, solar panels, windmills, worm bins, … and I could go on. The point is that if you are interested in incorporating off-the-grid materials into your own home, you can visit this "pavilion" and see firsthand how it would work, what maintenance it entails, and so forth. In addition, this pavilion is designed to have people come together; I believe this will help to reshape communities and restart local economies.

I have written a little story to help visualize this whole plan a little better.

Imagine, if you will, being able to drive into any small town and see a large chimney stack in the air. Imagine a large windmill next to it spinning wildly in the wind. Now imagine that those two things are just as synonymous with "green" as the Golden Arches are to McDonald's. Anyone who sees these two things while driving in any Midwest town will know that they can follow these giant towering images in the sky and go to a place that is classy, great for the environment, and is geared toward economic growth in a young, fun, and hip way, so that anyone can participate.

As you pull up to this beautiful place full of foliage and cobblestone walkways, you notice the small buildings. Little stone cottages have building integrated solar panels on their roofs. Small cobblestone walkways from each building leading to a central patio that holds the large outside fireplace with a tall chimney stack. People sitting outside in the patio, enjoying the fire, sipping on coffee in comfy chairs, and reading the daily paper.

As you pull in, you find that you have the option to park or drive through for a quick cup of coffee at the coffeehouse where they only serve the finest in organic, fair-trade coffee. Let us park instead, to check out this "town square," so to speak; Right here in front starting at the coffeehouse.

There is foliage inside as well; this place has chosen to use warm, inviting colors, yet the lighting is bright, for those who are here to work on their laptops. It doesn't feel dark, just cozy; the leather couch and chairs around the fireplace verify this feeling. The decor is very unique. The Constitution, Bill of Rights, and the Declaration of Independence have been enlarged and placed on the walls for easy reading. What a conversation starter, huh? At the counter, you can find literature and pamphlets from various energy companies, as well as the pavilion itself. These show detailed information on how easy it is to incorporate going green into your own home or business. They also explain how every building and business in this cluster has used and still practices green ideas in their building structures as well as their everyday business practices. This literature also states that every staff member has been educated on conserving energy and can answer many of your questions concerning any personal conservation needs you may have.

Now that it's your turn, you order a large caramel non-dairy macchiato. Why? Because you can! Plus, it sounds really good right now. The barista notices that you are new right away. She asks if you need help or if you would like someone to show you around. You tell her that you would rather go solo at the moment and will come back later with any questions.

Everyone seems so nice and friendly. The staff is smiling, engaging in conversations with their customers. People seem to have a good time here. Let's see what else this place has to offer. There is an exit through the back of the coffeehouse.

As you step outside, even more people are out on the patio enjoying the fire and their coffees. Wait just one minute—is someone over there eating a bowl of hot pasta? It's almost lunchtime and your stomach is growling. You close your eyes—mmmm—it even smells good. As you open them again, you look around. One of these paths leads to the right, straight into another cottage that is an Italian restaurant. Don't run, you tell yourself as you respectfully walk in, you can't make a fool of yourself now.

The atmosphere is just amazing; a beautiful, tall, slender fountain sits in the middle of the room with lighted vine growing up the middle. It makes the room seem serene amidst the constant chatter of the patrons. The tables surrounding the fountain are filled with businessmen and businesswomen, young couples, old couples, and a couple of college students with their backpacks hanging on the edge of their chairs. This place attracts the whole community and brings them all together in one place! How wonderful! On top of that, it's educational and great for the environment!

You are greeted by a beautiful young hostess and she lets you know that you are more than welcome to sit inside or outside and can move freely on the property, respectfully taking care not to pollute. Let's sit inside a moment, you sit down and say, "I'll make it easy on you. I want what the guy outside has with an iced tea please." She points out that we should still look at the menu for the helpful information about the company and what it stands for. If you wanted a tour, all you have to do is let your server know. The menu boasts the finest selection of wine in town. The menu explains that the portions may seem small, but lets you know that fast food has supersized us all. Smaller portions are healthier, but you also have the option of doubling your order if you choose to.

The menu offers everything from red meat, fish, salads, vegetarian entrees, and vegan-style meals. Your food arrives and you take the first bite and savor every Italian, tomatoey, garlic flavoring it offers. The menu excites you as you eat and, before you know it, you only have one bite left to eat and you keep it in your mouth for an extra second, swallow, have some tea, sit back a minute…and just take it all in. After you pay and leave a generous tip, you wander back outside. You feel enlightened; your tummy is full and warm. What else does this wonderful place have to offer? How do I learn more about what I can do about the environment? Can I really use what every business here uses in my own home? Where can I get it?

All of the sudden you hear angels singing and monks chanting. You get a warm and fuzzy feeling, followed by chills up your back—until you notice that it was just the outside speakers playing soft music for a more relaxed atmosphere. You look up again to see yet another path to the right. It's another cottage—let's go!

What a coincidence! This one is much smaller than the others are, but the staff is just as helpful and full of excitement as they teach you everything that you need to know about going green, saving the environment, and how to do it yourself at home! They also sell organic products such as vitamins and herbs for your well-being.

Wow, there is so much information you can't wait to get started! You give them your information to get started—and you are on our way! You leave feeling more educated and great that you will soon be making a difference in the world! Outside, you take a big sigh, and say, "Now what?" There is just one more building on this property that you might as well check out.

You walk in and—to your surprise—it's like an old English pub. You stop and look at your clock watch and notice that you have spent the whole day fiddling around and gabbing with the locals and now it's after five o'clock. Then you notice the ice-cold mugs, the half barrels on the wall behind the counter, and the burly looking tattooed bartender smiling from ear to ear like a big teddy bear. He says that he serves specialty micro-brewed keg beer from around the country. What are you to do but shrug your shoulders? The guy just twisted your arm so badly with his smile that you ordered a small mug.

You were thirsty anyway, right? He lets you know that you can go to the patio to mingle if you like. What a perfect way to spend a little more time with the locals.

You get your mug and finally head to the patio. It's nice here. There are also space heaters delicately placed to keep you warm if needed, but they are not eyesores. People are constantly coming up to you to engage you in wonderful, exciting conversations.

It is time for a cup of coffee before you leave—thank goodness for a drive through. How perfect to end the day in the pavilion and then to drive off with a souvenir? Now you can't stop thinking about the phone call you will receive when the energy company comes to the house to give you an estimate. You can't wait to tell all of your friends about your experience and wonder if you can get one of these town squares in your own Midwest hometown.

As you drive off, you notice how every business and residence in town has started already. There are solar panels on every roof and hybrid cars everywhere you look. The city is clean and inviting and you can't wait to go back! You drive off with just a tinge of guilt as you step on the gas to leave in your big SUV.

CHAPTER 32

With each business plan that I write, I must go the extra step and research to the best of my ability every aspect of the plan. Since that research never stops, I'm still finding new knowledge around every corner. I am trying my best to do my part and be prepared for the worst. After starting on the oil, I completed two more plans to help build new communities. I have written a plan to rebuild local school systems bringing children of all ages into one classroom and encouraging the children to challenge the system with contradictory sources of reference compared to classroom textbooks.

I was thinking of the idea of philosophy again and think that I have come up with a solution to several problems... including my gifted child's boredom in school. He is much like his parents, questioning everything in school and often gets scolded for it. We must ask this very important question before we move on. What will this country do when we run out of money and our educational system essentially throws up all over itself?

Mothers around the country will band together and step up to open their homes for homeschooling children. Neighborhood classrooms will pop up on every street. We will need to do this if we truly want our children to successfully continue to be educated. It really is not as scary as it sounds. Homeschooling sites are found all across the Internet. Most office supply stores now carry homeschooling supplies with tests and standards to help you get on your way. Mothers can open up "private" schools and can get an idea of how to run it as a business by looking up daycare business plans on the Internet. I would say that you could just set it up as a daycare and then incorporate your educational plan in the mix, creating your own professional plan to open up a business. Mothers, make sure that you are as thorough as possible and do as much research as you can before you start. Once you start to ask the neighbors what they think of the plan and whether they would support you on it, you may just find that we can bring back the basic principles of capitalism back into our country and begin to take it back from our corrupt government.

Mothers, I must also ask that you take into consideration how easy this can possibly be if we bring an idea to the table that I call "Challenge the System." For every subject taught in our public classroom, the curriculum only allows one way of teaching, usually following a certain textbook that only offers certain opinions. It is well known that there are flaws in every textbook. I suggest learning what the textbook has written and allowing the students to keep a separate notebook to allow them to research the subject on the Internet. At the end of each lesson, have the child do a presentation or report in front of the class for discussion. Having open, unbiased debates in class means more children will want to get involved—if only out of curiosity.

Challenging authority on a civil scale such as this will allow a child much more stability and respectability as an adult. Having the "teacher" also learn how to conduct their class in proper debate techniques such as learning how to control your emotions during a debate and getting your point across in a civil fashion. If the child does not produce a report or presentation, he/she should be segregated and not participate in the discussion—only being allowed to ask questions. This would also give a child the initiative to participate. Such as "Johnny, if you have not produced a report, how can you make a factual statement such as "such and such"? If you have a question that you can form from your statement, we would gladly accept it." This would challenge the child to think and should make him want to produce a report the next time.

Self-knowledge is the key to actual learning. You can tell a child all you want about a subject, but there is no guarantee he will learn it. If you challenge a child to learn on his own, I guarantee the results will be amazing. An adolescent is only human and all children are rebellious—it is in our nature.

Let's teach them how to do so in a proper civil manner, and the implications for a better and brighter future for mankind as a whole are on an enormous scale. I believe we will need to split our children into two age groups and keep them in separate rooms or have more than one "private" school per neighborhood. Children from the ages of three to six should be kept in a different classroom setting due to the maturity levels of these children. Children from the ages of seven to eighteen can be held in another. Of course, we must take age into consideration in initial teaching techniques, but we will have to adjust that scale as the younger ones move up. Each generation will be more and more educated. This will also educate everyone involved—students, teachers, and parents. Challenging the system as a parent is also very gratifying; getting parents involved in their child's homework to help challenge the system won't be very hard.

With one-room schoolhouses teaching children of many ages in one classroom, the same curriculum will blossom each child's mind. I believe you can teach high school history lessons to a child as young as seven and then give that child age-appropriate work, allowing the older children in the class to help teach the younger children. If you gain knowledge and are unable to teach another that knowledge, then what knowledge did you really gain?

If you are a mother considering this option for income in the future, you must keep in mind the depression, and what folks are able to afford. Have the children bring a sack lunch from home. Having bake sales and promotions to help out the "private" school will take a much bigger place within our communities.

CHAPTER 33

The third plan that I have written is about taking over healthcare with a plant that you can grow in your own backyard for free. This book is a major part of all of this—planting a seed in the minds of many to help revolutionize our lives and survive what is to come. These are very simple, common-sense solutions that are very possible to carry out by anyone wishing to use them. I want to be able to lay out the steps in which to take and give simple ideas to the public to be able to carry out as communities when this vision, this knowledge, and this absolute truth that I feel plays out.

On a recent trip I took with my husband, I met a man who posed a question to me that I have been unable to stop thinking about. "If you had an unlimited supply of marijuana, what would you do with it?" I told him immediately that I would cure myself and find a way to cure others as well. He laughed lightheartedly and then politely told me that it would never work. I have not stopped thinking of a solution. I had not ever considered having an unlimited supply. Since it is so very hard to come across, the thought had never occurred to me.

I have now decided to come out with my story and share it with the world. I must write a book explaining my past medical experience and my miraculous recovery. At the end, I plan on giving my gift to humanity with the creation of the Cannabis Cancer Treatment Center. I will offer a fairly detailed business plan, so that those who may be interested in opening one up in their own community may do so.

"Spreading knowledge and truth, allowing us to teach you to fish, so that you can eat for life."

The CCTC will guarantee nothing. The patients will be able to make any personal guarantee that they see fit. The patients will also be allowed to submit any dislike with the program that he or she chooses. Each client will be encouraged to make a personal video diary or journal during their stay. The CCTC will provide a small room for the private sessions to take place.

Each patient will have the choice to stay for one week for $5,000 or a twenty-eight-day stay for $30,000—depending on the patient's personal budget. Each price range is far cheaper than any other specialized center or hospitalization during that length of time. With more research, we will see if those prices are feasible, but off of the top of my head, that sounds about right for what it would take to run the CCTC.

Each client will be helped through proper nutrition, exercise, and rest. With a one-week stay, the client and a caregiver will be educated about cannabis, how it works medically, how to ingest, and personal responsibility on medicinal use. Also included during the first week will be monitoring doses and finding manageable amounts per individual—allowing them to rest and sleep as often as needed. If a one-week stay is all a person's budget will allow, they can be sent home with a diet and exercise regimen recommended by an on-site personal trainer and nutritionist that will be specific to the client's personal needs. They will meet with the house physician to work out a dosage plan for the new medication before returning home. The patient can then continue their journal if possible with a goal of at least eight entries—one for each day they are at the center and one twenty-eight days after initial treatment.

If an entire twenty-eight-day stay is possible, then the first weeks' regimen is no different. During that first week, the patient is educated in nutrition and exercise in a very hands-on way alongside that person's caregiver. The caregiver may choose to leave after the first week, making weekly visits from the time they leave to learn an overview of the week's activities.

The CCTC will allow the patient to learn how to cook alongside a dietitian, with a hands-on approach—from going to the store and learning what foods to choose and why to being able to ask questions and learn along the way. They will return to the CCTC to learn how to prepare and eat the food properly without losing precious vitamins and minerals. The patient will be encouraged to visit the spa and the gym at least once during that first week.

During the second week, the client will visit the gym with a personal trainer to work with his or her personal needs, regulating exercise at a tolerable level. This will allow the person to set small personal goals to meet and accomplish at their own pace. There will be time for pampering, massaging, scrubbing, or steaming at the spa to help relieve stress and tension from painful illnesses. Patients will learn how to care for their body and love the skin they are in.

During the third week, we will be moving the patient outside for organic horticulture, light exercise, such as hiking, bike riding, or just strolling around. They will keep scheduled appointments at the gym and spa.

On the fourth week, the patient will be observed as personnel will be able to step back and coach, making sure the patient will be able to stay healthy upon the return home.

The CCTC will host a final celebration at the end of each month inviting family for a final graduation dinner and congratulating everyone's successes and achievements. We will be bringing back folks from the first week to join us in the graduation dinner.

The CCTC will then close its doors for one week to clean, restock, and complete any researching on new patients for the new month. Privacy will be upheld with high honor; the research would involve any special needs that need to be addressed so that each person will be able to have a true personal experience.

Estimated costs for this project by the client will be all inclusive. Maintaining a garden on site and providing fresh meat with local livestock will help economically on top of being completely self-sufficient and off the grid—initially paying for building materials and eventually in a short period of time only needing to supply payroll as loans are paid off.

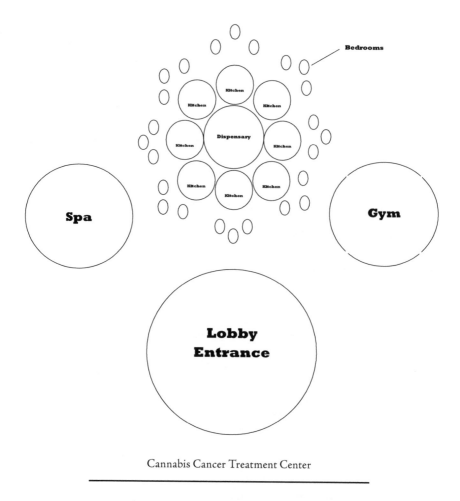

Cannabis Cancer Treatment Center

The staff of the CCTC will be trained and certified by the organization having a full time physician on staff. Each CCTC should employ at least thirty-two people, including eight personal trainers, eight nutritional therapists, five spa employees, five dispensary employees, and five lobby employees

The CCTC will have a twenty-four patient occupancy, allowing forty-eight beds so that caregivers can stay with the patient. The income should be enough for what we need and give opportunities to those who may need help based on income, opportunities to expand and grow, create jobs, and establish healthy and flourishing communities.

Building materials will consist of concrete domes that will easily blend into any landscape, allowing the beauty of nature to help cleanse the soul. These domes will be embedded into the earth, helping to provide privacy and discretion to our patients. Each dome will be connected by a tunnel; each will have an emergency exit; and topside decks will be placed throughout.

The CCTC is not currently worried about vacancies becoming a problem any time soon. The occupancy will be controlled by appointment only, picking a secure and discrete site for the safety and confidentiality of our patients. Unfortunately, this will only allow a select few at the center at a time, but with an open business plan, we hope to soon have as many as possible, helping to nudge the revolution in full force.

CHAPTER 34

We must be resilient, jump up, and **never** let any person, organization, corporation, or government take over our lives. I have become so very passionate the more and more I learn about politics and government. Not only on a federal level, but on a local level as well. Corruption is thick everywhere you look, and going to local town meetings is no exception. Socialism is already here in our backyards. I challenge anyone to find any given high school handbook that is written by our government-run public school system. I then challenge any one person to be brave and actually ask several teenagers about rules and regulations they may find "out of the norm" in regard to their own personal liberties. Please be aware that you may open up a can of worms, because what you may find is just a preview of what the beginning of this new era will bring if we don't put a stop to it immediately!

The *key* is being self-sufficient. It's not the "Green Movement" filled with carbon credits and crazy taxes. The "Green Movement" is just another way for the already existing rich to become much wealthier—a new stock market to play with and make money on. Learning how to become and converge to being self-sufficient will not be easy. We must learn how to grow our own food. Stop buying anything other than organic. Learn how to create our own energy to run our homes and transportation. Find ways to recycle water, trash, and everyday household items. Becoming off the grid will be the goal.

If we can create our own energy for our homes and our transportation, and no longer need to be on a government-run, corporate electrical grid or water supply, we would not need the government!

If we can teach our own children in our own communities and have neighborhood schoolhouses instead of giant tax-sucking, public, government created system, we would not need the government!

If we can heal ourselves by growing our own medication for disease and illness, at almost no cost, we would not need the government!

**Do you really need your government to hold your hand?*

If you really want freedom—if you truly want to be the leader of your own self—this is what needs to be done. It must include a movement, a massive group of folks who believe in our Constitution and that "We the People" should control the government and that the government should never control the people! I have done extensive research on politics, what my rights are as a citizen, and who is the best person to support politically. When I had my vision, the presidential candidacy was just beginning. I was sick and I spent hours and hours on research. I had to first find out what the difference was between a Republican and a Democrat. I didn't look up any definition to read and try to decipher. I just listened to each candidate to find similar solutions to problems. In short, at the time, most candidates said the same things. I watched most lie through their teeth and get away with it! Only one candidate stood out for me. Only one man made any sense to me. It was a man who was a doctor. He was a successful ob-gyn and had seen the corruption in the government. He decided to get involved as a concerned citizen. He ran for president in the 1984 elections and decided to step out of politics for a while shortly after and go back to his practice. He returned to politics ten years later in 1994. He, the congressman from Texas, was at one time on the Constitutionalist Party. He then went to the Libertarian Party, and then he was pushed to run for the 2008 Presidential Race. He simplified his beliefs by going back to the *core* principles of the original Republican Party and pointing out that the rest of his constituents were on the wrong path. That the two parties had melded into one neo-con party.

He was reluctant, so a huge grassroots effort formed to support him. I decided to do more research about him, and he was the only politician seeing what I was seeing. Our government has taken many rights away from us already, and we were going down a bad path as far as our nation was concerned. This congressman from Texas, Ron Paul, has earned a top spot on my own personal bucket list. I came to find out that this man practiced what he preached; his voting record is impeccable, and if he does not agree with a bill, then he votes against it—even if he is the sole person doing so. He sticks by his beliefs in the Constitution and the absolute right to freedom and liberty.

Ron Paul is now one of my personal heroes along with Rick Simpson. If I must go into politics, I want to learn from the best. Ron Paul has come up with a great vision of his own. He is using his www.campaignforliberty.com Web site to teach everyday citizens who are concerned with where our country is headed to understand the Constitution, law, and politics so that we can vote those who are currently corrupt in our system out and replace them with honest, informed people that are lovers of liberty. He has created an *enormous* following—regardless of his mainstream media snubbage.

With this organization—and many others like it—we really can win this fight for freedom! The revolution has already begun and people are "waking up" in droves! I have a deep-down feeling that I am not the only one that has been *chosen* and given knowledge or truths. I believe people all over the world have had similar experiences and are shrugging the knowledge off as something crazy, as I once did. Thousands of people who are too afraid to even speak of it.

These *chosen* few must come forward. We all must help humanity rebuild and renew. I believe that each one of us plays a vital role in what is to come. If you have an uncontrollable nagging feeling to get involved, *do it!* When the time is right, tell many of your own vision and feelings. Don't be afraid of what others may think of you! If this feeling is anything comparable to my own, I feel an urgency that won't go away. I feel as if I'm not doing enough! I feel pushed to write these things down—that is out of character for me. I must do this—even if I will be labeled as a crazy person by doing so! That is even better in my mind, if you think about it. I encourage you to question everything!—everything in this book! I dare you to research for yourself on the Internet. Take your next day off from work and spend one measly day of your life looking at information. Keep in mind that everything is opinion—even this book is just my opinion. Look at the information and take what you need from it. Make up your own mind and think for yourself! Use common sense and you will find what you need.

Think of it this way, there is one group of people that the government has always promised to take under its wing and help out on every aspect of their lives—from housing to healthcare. I wonder what a Native American would tell you about how well they now have it in the end with all of this government assistance?

I support Ron Paul if he is to run in the 2012 campaign for the presidency. He has a very real chance to win the 2012 election against Sarah Palin. I admire Ron Paul, and I know I will meet him someday. I am on the edge of my seat with excitement at the very thought!

I really should end this crazy chapter—even though I have much more to say. Politics has become a passion to me. What can I say? Before I bring it to a full close, I *must* quote Jeffrey Winterbourne from London University, who wrote this article called *"Our Right to Shamanism."*

"In the beginning, the shamans were the guides and leaders of humanity before we fell into current history and now at the end of time, the shamans are re-emerging to show the way. A shaman is someone that uses hallucinogenic plants to step outside of oneself, to oversee the situation, to stop time and discover new truths and metaphors, truths that have been suppressed from us through our cultural conditioning, truths that will redress the balance and harmony of all things. The shaman goes forth and returns with these illuminations and divine gems of true wisdom. A Shaman returns with these truths and then shares them with society in order to raise the consciousness of all.

Those that are meant to, should Shamanise, because a shaman is someone that has seen the end, therefore knows how it all works out, and is able to take their place on the cosmic stage without anxiety, without fear, without the programmed and restrictive conditioning inherent in our culture and to be free to find what is destined for us all; the true nature of our being—enlightenment."

CHAPTER 35

July 24, 2009

I have been feeling so well that lately I have been cheating on my diet. I have eaten hamburgers and a fantastic medium-rare steak! I have even been eating Peppermint Patties! I have been paying the price. I need to take this as a serious lesson. I need to be smart about how I treat my new life and my new body. I need to fully realize that the crap I went back to is not good for my body in any way and that it is possible that fast food and junk have contributed to my body being sick. I need to be aware that my body is not the same as it once was before I was sick—many of my parts are now gone. I really need to take care of my body this time around! I keep thinking that because of the oil's regenerative properties, if I keep taking this for the rest of my days, could it be possible to actually re-grow the organs that were removed? Scientists have found ways to re-grow organs—the human ear can grow on the back of a lab rat. Have they known these properties of the THC oil? If they do, are they trying to mimic it? So many questions! A simple plant has such a simple solution! Imagine the possibilities!

Let's just say we live in a perfect world, (just a sec) and everyone in the world could agree at the same time to implement the oil in everyday practices immediately at each physician's discretion. Could we make a concentrated saline and THC mixture to pour over wounds during surgical procedures?

Could we make a mixture using the THC that would be specially formatted for burn victims? THC oil is safe enough to make for over-the-counter sales and could be put into ointments for insect bites or beauty products. The amount of products and the amount of small businesses being able to pop up from the fruits of a plant that they can grow, cultivate, and transfer into a variety of products, projects, and ideas, on their own, will be enormous! I truly believe that anything is possible with this oil. I can't wait for others to come out and share their experiences with the oil. I hope that this book will inspire those that are sick, depressed, and in need to try my method—or in bulk like in the movie if you can—take their life into their own hands! Eat right and heal themselves! Teach your children the truth! Learn from the mistakes that I have made! Find out what regimen works best for them, and then spread the word!

I have had that red meat stuck for a full week and finally passed a large amount of it this morning. It is still up high in my abdomen in the same spot that I've been having problems with. From now on, I am going to try to stick to fish and chicken. I will try to introduce even more fruits and vegetables into my diet and treat my body as a temple to be more aware of myself and to be more in control of self-indulgence. I don't feel that I can afford that luxury.

CHAPTER 36

August 2, 2009

I am still battling my blockage. The last few days have been painful, and I look pregnant again. It kind of looks cute with this tiny little body. LOL! I weighed myself at my mom's house yesterday—because I don't believe in scales—and am back down to 110 pounds. The way my stomach feels today, I don't know that I will be able to eat much. I will need to go and get some generic Ensure to make sure that I don't lose any more weight. I try to find a high-protein and high-calorie drink. Since the chocolate flavor is not bad and is made with soy, it is safe for me to drink.

I am such an *idiot*! This whole time, I was feeling so much better and I was cheating on my diet. I was just careless and was caught in the moment of being alive and being able to have the things I had cut out of my life for so long. I hope I'm back on track and can get to feeling better soon! Look at me being such a whiner again! I am still 100 percent better than I once had been. This discomfort I am now going through is just a little speed bump, so I'll slow down for just a while. As soon as this stuff works its way out and this scar tissue is loose, I'm speeding my ass to the finish line as fast as possible! This book will be my way of "mooning" everyone in the system once I've crossed and won the race!!! LMAO!

CHAPTER 37

An old friend just moved back to town and came by to visit. I was letting her know how I had been and what I'd been doing. She was absolutely astonished that I had just recently gotten better. She looked at me and said, "Wow. The way you look, I assumed you'd been better for years." This is the same gal that, years ago, I almost donated a kidney to and felt like such an asshole when I did not. Not long after that incident, I was sick with Crohn's.

Little does this woman know that our encounter in life years ago has inspired me to be strong and fight throughout the years. I truly believe that things happen for a reason and it has all just "clicked" and came full circle. I will try to explain.

In long talks with this woman years ago, I asked questions about her illness and how hard it was for her to go to dialysis all the time. She is a very strong woman—much stronger than I ever was. Pain medication has never worked for her. She has had many surgeries, opting out for pain medication explaining "what's the point". Her veins in her arms have had to be replaced and her arms are full of scars. She talked about her illness as if it was no big deal. I remember her telling me in the car on the way to a transplant class that if she was ever given chemo or started to lose her hair, that she would shave it off after the first signs. She explained that to bypass the severe depression that could be caused by slowly watching your hair come out in large clumps. She suggested shaving it all at once and getting over the shock quickly so you can focus on getting better instead of feeling sorry for yourself and getting depressed. Can you imagine pulling out so much hair while applying shampoo that you would have to put a trashcan next to the shower so that you wouldn't stop up the drain? That would be depressing!

That story and her courage have always been with me. When I had gotten sick, I would remember our time together, and this story always made me aware that at any given moment, another soul out there has still got it worse than I do, and that if you are always aware that depression can be hard to avoid, *but it is possible.* I thought of her and her fighting spirit throughout my disease up until the very end. There were times that I got knocked down, but I fought so hard to get back up—and I always did!

In the end, before I had started the oil, the pain was so intense and would not let up that depression was imminent. It took hold, and I was ready to embrace death like a cozy blanket made of the love and warmth of the heavens. I still always had hope, and I never gave up! I still pulled out that vaporizer instead of giving up and doing nothing! I still kept trying the oil—even though I felt nothing for the first three days! I just kept going because that is all you can do... is just keep going; **Never stop trying! Never give up! Never surrender!**

When she was at the house recently, I put some of my face cream with the oil in it on her arm. The scars are so thick and it is so painful that she was unable to fully extend it. The pain was gone immediately and she was able to fully extend her arm with no pain! I hope that I can teach her how to fish so that she can eat for life! I look forward to it! I can't wait to repay the woman I looked up to for so many years. I once gave her hope, but I was an asshole and failed her. In hindsight, if the transplant had gone through, I might not have made it—or even worse, we both may have died. I am confident that this oil will fix her up as well!

I can't wait for the moment that she first realizes that she *will* live a long life and that she *will* be able to watch her children grow up—that she may even **live** long enough to see grandchildren someday! That moment, that thought, that realization when you **know** that you are okay that is absolutely priceless! I want to give that to her. I want to share my knowledge. I want to give her peace from the *hell* she doesn't even know exists—until it will be gone.

Free speech in the First Amendment of our Constitution is getting me through writing this journal, and I hope to put it all in a book to give to the world. The funny part is that—until I am finished with this book and get it published—I am too afraid to get caught. I am too afraid of even my local law enforcement to stand in a park and actually utilize my free speech right. Keeping this underground for now is a must. When this book gets published, I hope all who read this wake up and take their own lives into their own hands. I hope we can all stand up together as a unified movement and nation to tell our government to stay the hell out of our personal lives!

In writing this journal, I have tried to be anonymous, intentionally being vague about names and places. I don't think that is possible. I must come out and speak out. I must go public. How can I ask any of you who may be currently reading this to be brave and speak out unless I have the balls to do it myself?!

"But let it not be said that we did nothing. Let not those who love the power of the welfare/warfare state label the dissenters of authoritarianism as unpatriotic or uncaring, Patriotism is more closely linked to dissent than it is to conformity and a blind desire for safety and security.

Understanding the magnificent rewards of a free society makes us unbashful in its promotion, fully realizing that maximum wealth is created and the greatest chance for peace comes from a society respectful of individual liberty."

—Dr. Ron Paul

CHAPTER 38

August 3, 2009

Finally! This morning has brought some much-needed relief! I have been vigorously rubbing the homemade lotion on my tummy. I have been eating right and taking care of my body. The scar tissue in my abdomen is so thick and there is so much. I have no clue when I will be able to claim that I am completely cured, but I know it will be soon! Not only have I been using my lotion more often, but I'm in the final stages of complete disintegration of the evil boil that has riddled my face for almost a year now. I knew it was caused by a sinus infection, and I have an infected tooth on the same side of my face. To top it off, I started to get a bad ear infection on that same side. So, I put fresh oil on the boil every morning. I take a little and have had to put it on the inside of my nose to get it closer to the seed of the boil. I could feel the medication spread through my sinuses and was able to breathe better. I also put oil on floss and put it on all my teeth, and I also went and got some waxed ear cones to light and pull out earwax to help with drainage. I think the combination of those things really did the trick! My sinuses, neck, ears, and teeth all feel so much better! I don't know if there is anything this oil cannot do?

I need to start doing some research on physicians. I won't be able to approach just any physician about this oil and its properties. This movement needs the medical community to wake up! We need physicians that believe in free enterprise—those that take their Hippocratic Oath seriously and are willing to go underground if necessary and become "house doctors." This movement needs caring and loving medical professionals that are in their profession because they love it and truly want to help heal and preserve human life. I know these people exist—I've seen it.

This country is going to be in such poverty that many of these physicians will receive payment in food such as fruits, veggies, livestock, and so forth. I'm sure that there will be imposters, but I want you to think about whether you need your government to regulate everything in your life or if are you smart enough to make your own decisions. Being poor will make you more inclined to research your own symptoms before calling a doctor. Talk with others and find out for yourself which doctor will have the best reputation. Credentials such as diplomas will soon mean nothing because anyone can print one off. When this monster Depression comes, people won't be able to afford college. On-the-job training will be how we learn, and most of that will need to be done underground. Humanity will band together, and knowledge will start to flow. Apprenticeships will be very common for many occupations and subjects. An entire underground system of teaching others will explode! We will not be brought down! We will all make this new world a better place—full of community, family, love, and pride in country! Question everything! You won't be able to sue for damages—even the physicians won't have the money.

It's bad enough now that we trust our system so much that we do whatever our doctors tell us to do—we put pills and drugs into our bodies that are harmful with "the hope of feeling better." They even tell you how harmful it is in a way that doesn't sound so bad because of that possibility that it may work. You are not given natural alternatives—you are given poison and invasive surgeries. Do you know why? It's the phrase I just used—"the hope of feeling better." I don't think that in all my years and the many doctors that I encountered, not one used the word "heal" when it came to treating my illness. The only time that I was ever told I could "heal" or concentrate on healing was after an invasive surgery. Doctors are taught to treat symptoms and ease your pain.

We no longer need any of it, do we? With this oil, almost anyone can be a doctor. Communities will come together and help each other. Natural healers (of which will be many of you) will be able to heal each other of afflictions. Medical gardens will start to grow with herbs from all over the world. Medical victory gardens will be in the backyards of many! Neighbors will be helping neighbors teach each other, helping the tree of knowledge grow very tall with many thick branches.

I was once told by a banker—when I was declined (yet again) for a loan on my pavilion—that the public has no interest in knowledge and they don't want to be taught anything when going into an establishment. All I could think was *Wow! These people actually believe that the public or the masses are stupid. That we are not smart enough to make our own informed decisions. Of course we want to learn! Those that don't will not survive—those that do, understand the importance of knowledge and will gladly absorb as much as possible.*

Folks who look at the public as simple cattle are in for a rude awakening. How dare they assume that we are not capable of being in charge of our own lives and that we are too slow to make our own decisions! Knowledge is out there! Information is everywhere! You should never push information on someone unwilling to hear it. They will only continue to be "asleep." Knowledge must be obtained by self-pursuance. Plant a seed and, at the first sign that they look uncomfortable, just let it go. From that point on, they will be more vigilant and start to notice for themselves the real happenings of the world.

CHAPTER 39

August 7, 2009

I awoke this morning with a certain clarity. I am faced with two choices. I either stay hidden and try to get the word out anonymously, which all of my family wants for me. My family is concerned for me, and rightly so, since I am as well. If I were to be incarcerated, I would be without my medication and would end up dying a slow and painful death in martyrdom. I have no interest in that at all! I didn't fight for all of these years to watch my children grow up—only to have them ripped out of my hands!

My next choice is to go public. If I choose the path I'm pushed to go, I must go really public! I must finish this book and send it to every public source I can think of. I must send this to politicians and news media alike. I must get over being a scared little girl and just do this! I must not care who judges me or how! I need my fellow Americans to wake up! Listen and stand up for themselves! I will need my fellow patriots to stand by my side and support me—lest I be food for hungry wolves. I think a part of me has been waiting for someone else to do this, but I feel I can wait no more. If I don't stand up, who will?

Rick Simpson is doing what he can in Canada, and his knowledge of the oil has spread worldwide! I'm sure that this man has already saved thousands of lives. Let's all stand up as a unified movement and demand to be able to save ourselves! We truly have a real possibility to save millions of lives if we stand together as a nation and demand true freedom! I had chills as I watched the news this morning. I would almost find it amusing if it were not true.

As you may know, CNN is a Democratic-run news station and FOX is a Republican-run news station. FOX has started to report on town hall meetings of citizens who are afraid to lose their freedoms in the healthcare battle. The more-than-one-thousand-page bill of socialized healthcare is about to go to a vote, and citizens are demanding that it be read. They cannot believe (myself included) how our elected officials can vote properly without reading the damn bill! If you are elected to do a job, and if you are paid to do a job, why would you not do it? Dun ... Dun ... Dun! Corruption!

CNN, however, has reported that organized angry mobs just want to be on television to stop this wonderful healthcare plan. The White House has started to ask the American public for help. They actually came out and said that if you receive an e-mail that in any way was worded against the government or its healthcare plan, to forward it to the White House so that it can be looked at. Excuse me?!! I have never heard of such an invasion of privacy! I have never heard of our government trying to have other citizens actually turn others in for free speech! What is wrong with everyone?!! When will we all wake up and finally see before it is too late?!! CNN has announced that the DNC plans on sending busloads of fifty-plus individuals to invade these local town meetings! What happened to the word local!? Where is the democracy in that!!? ... This would be the true ugliness of politics sticking out its ugly head.

CHAPTER 40

August 9, 2009

I wonder if others are having a huge struggle within themselves, as I do. I don't really feel crazy, but I think I am still hung up on what others may think. I have started to also read a bit more of the Bible. I started in the New Testament. I want to find out what Jesus did and how he was able to heal miraculously—if only I could find more on the woman.

This is really weird. I was just interrupted writing in this journal because my youngest just woke up. He told me that he had a dream about a flower and that the flower was on fire. I asked him if it was scary and he said no. He said he spit on the flower and the flower grew in the fire and the fire got bigger. I said "Oh, my," and he said the flower could talk; so I asked, "What did the flower say?"

He buried his face in my shoulder and was being flirtatiously shy, shaking his head and smiling. He said, "I don't remember"

I asked, "Did you talk to the flower?"

He smiled again flirtatiously and said, "I told it that I loved it."

So I smiled very big myself and asked, "Did it love you back?"

Flirtatiously again, burying his head in my shoulder, he nodded yes.

Out of nowhere, I told him as I hugged him tight I said, "Honey, I think you just talked with God."

He smiled and I set him down. After another bear hug, I said to him, "Don't forget your dream. ..."

He cut me off and said he wanted some cereal and that told me he was ready to be done talking about it, so now, he is inside eating his cereal, content as can be.

Yet, I find the timing strange since I was just doubting my sanity. I just realized that this instance must be a sign. I need to roll up my sleeves and dive into this new life I am to lead. I am now going to have to research not only the New Testament of the life of Jesus, but also what it says about Moses and the burning bush he spoke to as well. My mind is racing and my heart is pumping. This is *real*—this is *really* happening!

We don't even pray at home. I used to have my oldest pray at night before bed, but have fallen out of that habit. We have not done so with the youngest yet. I believe it may be time to reaffirm, reinforce, and encourage a relationship with both of my children and God. This journey my family and I are about to embark on is going to be one hell of a ride. I must prepare and harden my heart from false rumors and from others that may say that I am off my rocker. We can overcome and accomplish anything as a family and a nation—as long as we stand up for ourselves and demand a truly free choice for ourselves in the name of personal liberties.

I am trying to remember the prayer and how I taught my oldest to pray ...

"Oh Father who art in Heaven,
Hallowed be thy name.
Thy Kingdom come,
Thy will be done,
On Earth as it is in Heaven.
Give us tomorrow our daily bread,
And forgive our Trespasses as we will forgive those that Trespass against us.
Lead us not into temptation,
But deliver us from Evil."

Then we break, this is when you can tell God of your day and concerns. Always making sure to add our own verse that we came up with ...

"Thank you Lord, for the roof over our heads,

The clothes on our backs,
And the food in our tummies.
For Yours is the Kingdom,
The Power,
And the Glory Forever.
~Amen."

I have always felt that taking that break to discuss your day helps in having a real relationship with God. I would think it would be tiresome—if not boring—to hear only half-hearted prayers at night by some who may just be using repetition and not really connecting on the level needed.

I have a theory that the repetition in prayer is not needed. I have always prayed and talked to God with my heart—just as I would discuss any deepest thoughts and feelings with a friend in asking for help and guidance. I have also never believed that God is a spiteful God. I believe that God is love and the light of heaven. That God gives us the chance of knowledge, love, and the chance of true happiness within ourselves. He also gave us the power of choice and reason. I believe it is up to each individual to choose how he or she will live that gift of life they were given. For its purpose is for knowledge for our *soul* and the choices we make in this life *will be judged* by how we made each decision—whether it be for selfish reasons or if you have always done things for others and have been most unselfish in your decisions.

I am convinced that the concept of hell is what we live in on earth. That there is evil and bad out there around every corner. This is our great big classroom to learn and make mistakes—and learn from those mistakes. I am still on the fence when it comes to believing in an actual devil. I sometimes think that the devil was created to be able to *blame* our bad choices on or to be able to *blame* for things that have not gone well in a person's life. For some reason, I believe that blame is a very natural way to react to things not going your way. It is one of those primal instincts I think, that really is *not* that hard to overcome. Far too many people don't accept their own actions or just don't accept the fact that "shit happens" and feel that they must put blame on something—anything. Nothing can just be.

I think people need to realize that shit happens and there is no blame to be put. In most situations throughout your life—even if you try to place "blame"—it is pointless because you can't fix the past, no matter where you place the blame. Instead of placing blame on anything (if you come to that point), don't think of blame. Immediately find out what mistakes were made in that situation and learn from them. I believe everything happens for a reason. Even if you are not able to find a reason right after an incident, it will be revealed later and the knowledge gained from that experience will come back to help you in a different time in your life.

Not only do I not believe in organized religion, but I also do not believe in the concept of a chosen religion. I think different religions were created by God himself to give sight and inspiration to the human species. In having different views (our gift of choice), he purposefully created diversity. Without diversity in all things, how would we be able to learn and absorb the knowledge in all things? To find out our own truths with our gift of choice?

Now, don't get me wrong, I won't deny that it is a beautiful feeling that is created in the air on a Sunday morning church service. It is a wonderful thing that communities—if only for one day a week—gather together in harmony with good deeds and thoughts of peace, love, and gratitude. The air in any church has always been thick like fog filled with that feeling of love and peace—a serene calm.

It is the severe hypocrisy that I see out of the church and the choices that some people make who claim to be religious that is what saddens me. To those, church and religion can be a front to some who want to appear to be good in the eyes of the community. It is up to each individual to decide what is best for them. For, what you feel in your heart is always where you find absolute truth in yourself. Start to not only think with your brain, but with your heart as well, for if they do not work together, you may not be able to find peace within yourself. Open yourself up to gut feelings for they will help you find your way. Keep your morals high and stick with them. Be grateful for what you do have, and always help those who come before you, that come to you for aid. Be true to yourself and you will be true to others.

The Golden Rule really does apply in all situations!

"Do unto others as you would have done for yourself."

Start your day with compliments toward others, and the goodness will spread through the entire community. Listen to good and upbeat music to get your day started, and smile!

~ A frown will bring you down, but a smile will always last a longer while.

I don't mean to be preachy in any way, but I feel compelled to write down my views so that others can relate. I feel that I need to encourage people to find that feeling of love within themselves and let it consume the entire body. I encourage you to spread that feeling of happiness and content to others in these dark times. I also know that—even in politics—religion plays a key. As you may now know, my beliefs are simple yet really cannot be easily explained to those who are interested in my personal choices.

I beg of those who may put me on a religious pedestal to take me down! I am no saint and have many faults of my own. I have led my own life by my own morals and judgments and have made many of my own mistakes. I just hope that I have learned what I have needed to continue this life in a virtuous way and to continue to learn all that I can. I want to be able to always make informed and balanced decisions based on all truths that I can find in a field of falsehoods—just as I encourage others to do the same.

The point is ... that being a good person is not that hard. Making choices in your life with good intentions is simple and easy. We can all make a difference! My mother has always taught me that with every action there is a reaction. If the action is positive, it spreads. The same goes for negative actions. It is like dropping a stone in water and watching the ripples. Make sure to fill your stone with love, happiness, and good deeds and throw it as hard as you can into that water so that the ripples travel far and wide!

CHAPTER 41

August 18, 2009

My blockage up high is still present, but it has relaxed if only a little bit. A new friend of mine had suggested that I try to drink aloe vera juice. I recently purchased some, and I cannot believe the difference it has made. When I first tried it, I had put it in some juice. It tasted horrible because the mixture was fifty-fifty, but I drank it all the same. It felt as if I had lubricant running down my tummy. It felt *sooo* nice, and within two hours, I was able to have a bowel movement. I have since found that if you put the aloe vera juice in coffee, it hides the taste. The juice itself is bitter, and putting it in bitter coffee is a nice way to wake up in the morning.

Aloe Vera has many healing properties of its own. It benefits the immune system, it helps digestion, and increases absorption of anything you put in the body. Oh, think how nice it feels after a sunburn. ... I highly recommend it if you have digestive problems. Here is a note of caution, if you are still on prescription medication or take vitamins and so forth, be careful to monitor yourself because of the high absorption properties of the aloe vera. On the oil, however, I have very high hopes that it increases the potency of the oil in my body—due to the very minute amount I am able to produce.

I do believe that the rocks I passed were indeed the steak I had cheated on several weeks ago. Now the food is gone, but the scar tissue is being stubborn! …???Hmmm … I wonder if I should put fresh oil on my tummy and then rub it in with the lotion.? … I'll try it because I just feel uncomfortable—kind of like when you're in your last trimester and the baby is putting pressure on organs, making it uncomfortable to move around. The scar tissue is just so thick.

Our family was able to acquire one of those pull-up bars that hang on a doorjamb. This thing is awesome! Last week I was able to stretch and rip more away, and it has taken a full week to get over it. I felt the hot burning and ripping as I stretched. It feels great "in the moment," and I never know whether or not something will come loose. Depending on how much I rip away, it feels raw each time—as though I am recovering from a surgical procedure. When the cold chills hit … bed rest is what is needed.

This is my fourth month on the oil, and I am getting anxious about feeling "whole" again. I am being impatient. I know this could take me a full year to heal completely with this small amount of oil. Since it did take eight years of sickness, one year of healing is not a bad switch. I still hope to get a full two ounces of this stuff. The first time I watched "Run from the Cure," I was so depressed afterward because he used a full pound of marijuana to get only two ounces of oil. Where was I going to get a whole pound of weed!? On top of that, where was I going to make it? As soon as I found out that my vaporizer could produce the oil in small amounts, my entire world changed! I am so absolutely livid that—after all these years, the hell and pain that me and my family have gone through, and the money that was taken from my family—it took a fifty-dollar machine and a five-dollar spatula with a medicine that can be grown for free to *cure* me… Or at the very least put me in a remission that I have never experienced before! I can't wait until we can move our family out of this state.

I try not to go out of the house anymore. When I am in public and people see me, they want to know how I'm doing and what I'm doing. I try not to tell everyone and have gotten to the point that when they ask, I just tell them to watch the movie. I am so scared that this is getting out and my name is already out there. I need to try to hurry with this book and make it public. I fear that only the public can save me from the system. I hope and pray that I can do this as soon as humanly possible. I fear for my life and the safety of my family on a daily basis, but I still can't stop telling the truth! How can you keep your mouth shut when you know the remedy to all disease and illness? How can I sit idly by and watch others die needlessly without telling of Mr. Simpson's discovery and my method of retrieval.

I can't!—and neither will you once you have been helped by this oil or seen it help others with your own eyes!

I am going to go into detail about another healing miracle. The cap that I replaced has fallen out completely. Not only that, but when I was flossing with my oil, half of my tooth fell out on the counter. That is when I realized that I had a *very severe* infection. The entire left side of my face must have been infected for at least *two years*! This would explain the blackness that crept from those teeth to the middle of the roof of my mouth! I always thought it was from my Crohn's, but when I first started on the oil … it went away. This also gives new light to the boil and ear infection on that same side of my face for so long.

When that part of my tooth fell out, I felt the gigantic hole it left. Infection poured into my mouth and I could feel the pain when the air moved through my sinuses. I remembered that my dentist had given me a root canal on that tooth long ago. I have spent thousands of dollars to fix that side of my mouth. When he capped the root canal, the cap never stayed on longer than a few weeks. I have gone back several times. When I started to buy over-the-counter caps and put them in myself, they would last a few months instead of only a few weeks.

Anyhow, I burst into tears at the pain. My husband came to my rescue once again and drove to town to get me some gauze to put in my tooth. The entire time he was gone, I was pacing and freaking out because the infection was just pouring in my mouth and it took everything I had not to vomit. When he got home and I was able to make fresh oil, and I just smothered the gauze with it and shoved the gauze in the gaping hole at the roof of my mouth where the tooth had once been.

The oil calmed the pain instantly, and I could feel the medication spread through my sinuses to my entire face. I even felt it in my forehead, and everything in my head cleared within minutes. It was disgusting! I could feel the mucus fall to my throat like someone was suctioning it out of my face. It went on for an entire thirty minutes—I was having to spit in the trashcan every five. I felt drainage in my ears and actually heard the flub-flub of the drainage flowing out of my sinuses and ear canal. It was almost as if I was just drowning in it. After I prepared more oil, I took out the gauze. At the tip of the cotton was a tiny ball of nicotine gum stuck to the end. I had found the cause of the infection! Gum I had chewed to stop smoking—almost two years earlier—must have worked its way in there and fermented.

I have decided not to see the dentist just yet. It is now day three of the oiled-up gauze, and the hole is closing up just fine. My only concern at this point is that if the other half of my tooth breaks off. I may need to have a replacement or something so that I will not do further damage—even if it is just for cosmetic reasons. The infection seems to be gone, and the hole is slowly healing, but we will see what this stuff can do!

CHAPTER 42

August 26, 2009

Dangers of getting caught:
1. If you are in a state that does *not* recognize the medicinal effects of this plant, you are in real danger.
2. If you are in a state that *does* recognize the healing properties of the plant, you are still in real danger.

The first danger is almost too self-explanatory. Depending on what state you live in, you can literally lose your entire life for getting caught with any small amount of the plant—including seeds and paraphernalia. Check out norml.com for a complete map of states with links to laws and regulations concerning your state. My state has a no-tolerance policy.

If the stats are true according to norml.com, one in four Americans smokes cannabis. This means that the people who want to use it already do—and have just learned how to hide it. The only physical harm to your body would be done if you got caught by authorities. Not all police officers are bad people. As I have found out for myself over the years, I believe that many are just men who like the feeling of power. It is really no secret that, statistically, large numbers of police officers are guilty of domestic violence. Not all peace officers are bad... but the good ones are becoming few and far between. The good ones are starting to retire, and the new young ones (within the past two years) are a whole new breed. Always have a guard up and always use your Fifth Amendment right if you are ever caught. I must insist that any novice who is considering this method watch videos made by Barry Cooper. He is a former DEA agent who realized the war on drugs was majorly on marijuana. He noticed the difference in raids between crack houses and marijuana violators. He noticed that when they busted a crack house, it was in the scummiest parts of town, the home was almost always unlivable, and it almost never happened without a fight. Most marijuana violators lived in residential neighborhoods and were willingly arrested in front of their families. He noted that these were good people and that their children were almost always bright or gifted. He realized that he was ruining good and decent people and has been helping the novice hide their "stash" from authorities for years now.

He has written several books and released many videos that you can easily find on YouTube or in other places on the Internet. He has other detailed videos and information for sale. He has excellent information for the lifelong cannabis user as well as any novice!

Secondly, if you are in a state that does recognize medicinal needs of the plant, you still are in real danger. The federal government still has a no-tolerance policy.

The states that have acknowledged the fruits of this plant have regulated the amount that can be made. Most of these states only allow around five plants to be grown on the patient's private property, so that you can have five stages of growth on the plant and have enough to last—and always have one ready to cultivate. That does not sound bad, and it sounds as if they are looking out for you and have your best interest at heart. Do not be *fooled*! With my research, you are lucky to get two or three ounces of bud off of a readily harvested plant. I think that the government has known about the oil since 1974 and knows that you would need fairly large amounts to get rid of an illness.

The law for the state of Colorado reads:

Proposed Amendments to Rules Pertaining to Medical use of marijuana (5 CCR 1006–2), Regulation 2—Definitions and Regulation 4—Change in applicant information. Revised April 30, 2009

Under Regulation 4-B: Change in applicant information. This states exactly: A patient who no longer has a debilitating medical condition as defined in Regulation six shall return his registry identification card to the department within twenty-four hours of receiving such information by his or her physician."

Regulation 6-B explains these conditions as cancer, glaucoma, HIV, severe pain, cachexia, severe nausea, seizures from epilepsy, or spasms from multiple sclerosis.

Regulation 6-D: "In making its determination the department will consider whether there is information that the proposed condition is chronic, debilitating, and may be specifically diagnosed and whether scientific evidence that treatment with marijuana may have a beneficial effect."

In short, this is what they have done, legalized too small of an amount to cure anything. If by chance you do cure your HIV, cancer, or whatever so-called "incurable" disease, you must immediately return your medical marijuana card—and by the way, any fees (around $100) are non-refundable by the state. This can all be done by a panel of people who may have never been sick or used the drug for benefits. This panel will get to decide whether or not you live in freedom or die in pain.

Here is my point. This revolution will not proceed unless we all unite and demand that this plant be used for medicine on a *grand* scale. No longer let *them* think for you! Think for yourself! We must take the seeds of this plant and spread it everywhere! In public parks, medians, and town squares! There is an organization dedicated to this effort in particular, called: Plant the Land. I believe that they also have networking sites that you can check out on myspace.com and facebook.com.

Can you imagine plants ... weeds taking over public areas? What better advertising for a revolution?! My hat goes off to these folks and all others who have already taken the steps to start this revolution. It really does take baby steps, but I believe we will learn to run before we walk! I believe that when this book is published, knowledge will spread. People around the world will read it and begin to think and do for themselves, building healthier, more educated communities, without government or corporate interference.

Grow your own and make it happen! If you are sick, I guarantee that you can find a family member who will be willing to help you learn and purchase—whether that be in a "legalized" state or not. If you are in a legal/decriminalized state, you may also learn at a dispensary. I believe that you can find pretty much any answer you need from the Internet, books, and magazines. Veer onto your own path and spread out your research so that you feel confident in your knowledge that you are learning and will be able to teach others that knowledge with ease. Make sure that they want or are willing to listen. Hand them this book and have them read it. Sit down at a laptop and play "Run from the Cure" for grandma with the book in hand to see if she wants to read it. There are so many ways to spread the knowledge, but you will not be able to force it.

Remember that self-sought-after knowledge is the *only* one that counts. If you start to say too much at one time and are overexcited, you might get those "crazy" looks that I have become accustomed to. I must constantly remind myself to say as little as possible and allow the other person to ask the questions. I have come to know when to back off and when to proceed. If they look the least bit interested, I will just recommend the movie, plant the seed, and let it be. That person must decide whether to nurture it or not.

CHAPTER 43

I have been working hard, researching, traveling, and writing this book. My mom and I took a mother-daughter trip to the mountains. I was hoping to find some help with my research for my book along with a publisher. I found myself in a local mountain shop and asked if this person had knowledge of the hemp oil. I had to explain myself and tell him that I was traveling to find anyone who would speak on the topic and that I had used the oil and written a book to share with the world. He very cautiously looked me up and down before he told me of a doctor who was also a professor at the University of Colorado in Colorado Springs who was researching the effects of medicinal marijuana on a human cellular level. We went back to the hotel we were staying at and started to research. I was able to find several sites that matched my search for Bob Melamede.

As I read his research and papers he had written, I came to my own conclusions. Here is how I interpret his research in a nutshell:

He explains that the human body naturally produces something called cannabinoids. These Cannabinoids are even in mother's milk to help the child to suckle after birth—and, yes, it is something each one of our bodies produce naturally. The cannabinoids are detrimental to the development and immune system of the human body, and every other mammal on the planet. Through the process of evolution, he concludes that the fact that governments around the world have outlawed and made a natural plant criminal to possess or grow...

... So, on an Earth which at one time had many different strains of a weed that grew very naturally in fields *all* over the world, has diminished on a *grand* scale.

In my own point of view, this has caused needless loss of our trees for paper, needless loss of oil for fuel, needless loss of fresh oxygen to be potentially made to clean our polluted air... I could go on. Dr. Bob explains that this has also caused humans around the world to diminish our own cannabinoids in our bodies through generations of elimination in our bodies through government-controlled evolution. Please read *The Emperor Wears No Clothes* and *101 Ways to Save the World with Hemp* by Jack Herer, a very intelligent man who has been in the movement and helped start this revolution years ago.

On a very basic level, the human body is riddled with different receptors in the brain and throughout the body that talk to each other to make the body work in harmony. The earth has provided our medicine from the beginning of time... Psalm 104:12 says, "He causeth the grass to grow for the cattle, and the herb for the service of man."

With more research on holistic medicine, I believe it works very similarly and is based on the fact that each plant or herb in the world will trigger different receptors in the body to allow our bodies to function in balance and harmony or homeostasis. Marijuana produces those cannabinoids that, in effect, work on every system in the body, producing homeostasis solely on its own. This plant has been used by the human species for so long that archeologists found the cultivated plant in a Chinese tomb dated to be at least five thousand years old. The contents show that the ancient Chinese used the plant for medicinal and psychoactive purposes. So *at least* five thousand years ago, this plant has been growing in many different strains around the world!

Dr. Robert Melamede—who is cool enough to go by "Dr. Bob"—says that we all make very naturally what he calls endocannabinoids.

Endo means "within," and *cannabinoid* means "marijuana-like lipid products or fat."

These endocannabinoids are able to regulate and balance every system in our entire bodies. When we consume the plant and or its products, our cannabinoid receptors are awakened within the body. Did you know that smoking cannabis will not cause lung cancer? There is a *huge* difference in the pharmacology of the compounds found in tobacco and those in cannabis. The concentrated oil is also an antimicrobial and antibacterial. When put into a Petri dish, you can watch germs and bacteria die around it. Cannabinoids will kill cancer cells while protecting healthy cells around it. Tumors found in the lung have been reduced or eliminated. Cannabinoids will also dilate our bronchial tubes to help asthma sufferers and others with respiratory problems. If you are a patient with respiratory problems, not only do I suggest the oil, but I also suggest that you use a vaporizer to get the vapor into the lungs without irritation.

Cannabinoids will also protect the brain and are found miraculous in the elimination and reduction of tumors on the brain as well. We also have CB1 receptors in our skin. Cannabinoids can also slow down the aging process. It can protect the heart and, when cannabinoids hit the bloodstream, our CB2 receptors jump into action. CB2 receptors are found in our white blood cells and regulate the immune system and the inflammatory response.

In just about all autoimmune diseases, the body is trying to go into overdrive. The immune system produces free radicals and treats the body by attacking itself. Consuming cannabinoids from the marijuana plant turns on those CB2 receptors, bringing a homeostatic environment within the body. This would also mean that it works on HIV and AIDS as well because it balances the immune system. I believe that by ingesting the concentrated oil with high amounts of THC, (Tetrahydrocannabinol) the cannabinoids will remedy the disease, cancer, or illness.

Rick Simpson said, "You can smoke it till the cows come home, but it won't be enough to cure ya."

Dr. Bob also explains that cannabinoids also help to alleviate pain and aide in sleep, in a natural way that is much safer on your body than even taking a simple aspirin.

This next bit of information I have been able to copy off of a blog that has since been taken down from the Internet, but I'm sure that you can find the same—if not more—by doing a search yourself. The author of this article is unknown. This is a repost with a few edits ...

"When Bayer introduced aspirin in 1899, cannabis was America's number one painkiller. Until marijuana prohibition began in 1937, the U.S. Pharmacopoeia listed cannabis as the primary medicine for over one hundred diseases. Cannabis was such an effective analgesic that the American Medical Association (AMA) argued against prohibition on behalf of medical progress. Since the herb is extremely potent and essentially non-toxic, the AMA considered it a potential wonder drug. Instead, the invention of aspirin gave birth to the modern pharmaceutical industry and Americans switched away from cannabis in the name of "progress." But was it really progress? There can be no doubt that aspirin has a long history as the drug of choice for the self-treatment of migraines, arthritis, and other chronic pain. It is cheap and effective. But is it as safe as cannabis?

History:

Marijuana has been used for over 5,000 years.
No one has ever overdosed on marijuana.
Aspirin has been used for 108 years.
Approximately 500 people die every year by taking aspirin.

The Law:

Marijuana is a Schedule 1 drug, meaning that the government believes it is extremely dangerous, highly addictive, and of no medical value.
Aspirin is available for pennies and can be purchased by children at any drug, grocery, or convenience store. Often they are just handed out for free by people with no medical education.

Marijuana Side Effects:

For two to four hours, marijuana can cause short-term memory loss, a slight reduction in reaction time, and a reduction in cognitive ability. (It makes you stupid for a little while.) These conditions *do not* persist after the herb wears off.

Hunger
Paranoia
Depression
Laughter
Introspection
Creative Impulse
Euphoria
Tiredness
Forgetfulness

Aspirin side effects:

When taken with alcohol, aspirin can cause stomach bleeding.
Reye Syndrome in children: fat begins to develop around the liver and other organs of the child, eventually putting severe pressure on the brain. Death is common within a few days.
People with hemophilia can die.
People with hyperthyroidism suffer elevated T4 levels.
Stomach problems include dyspepsia, heartburn, upset stomach, stomach ulcers with gross bleeding, and internal bleeding leading to anemia.
Dizziness, ringing in the ears, hearing loss, vertigo, vision disturbances, and headaches.
Heavy sweating
Irreversible liver damage
Inflammation and gradual destruction of the kidneys
Nausea and vomiting
Abdominal pain
Lethargy
Hyperthermia
Dyspepsia: a gnawing or burning stomach pain accompanied by bloating, heartburn, nausea, vomiting, and burping.
Tachypnea: Abnormally fast breathing

Respiratory Alkalosis: a condition where the amount of carbon dioxide found in the blood drops to a level below normal range brought on by abnormally fast breathing.

Cerebral Edema: Water accumulates on the brain. Symptoms include headaches, decreased level of consciousness, loss of eyesight, hallucinations, psychotic behavior, memory loss, and coma. If left untreated, it can lead to death,

Hallucinations, confusion, and seizure.

Prolonged bleeding after operations or post-trauma for up to ten days after last aspirin.

Aspirin can interact with some other drugs, such as diabetes medication. Aspirin changes the way the body handles these drugs and can lead to a drug overdose and death.

If you think that cannabis is actually safer than aspirin, you are not alone. In October 2000, Dr. Leslie Iversen of the Oxford University Department of Pharmacology said the same thing.

In her book, *The Science of Marijuana*, Dr. Iversen presents the scientific evidence that cannabis is, by-and-large, a safe drug. Dr. Iversen found that cannabis had "an impressive record" when compared to tobacco, alcohol, or even aspirin.

"Tetrahydrocannabinol is a very safe drug," she said. "Even such apparently innocuous medicines as aspirin and related steroidal anti-inflammatory compounds are not safe."

If safety is your concern, cannabis is clearly a much better choice than aspirin. If you eat it or vaporize it, it just might be the safest painkiller the world has ever known."

Dr. Bob also explains that cannabinoids bind with nerve endings and protect nerve cells from dying, thereby reducing pain. The protection in the brain can result in complete prevention of getting Alzheimer's disease.

"It cannot be over-emphasized that the action of any plant is always more than the action of any specific constituent chemical."—David Hoffman, Professional Medical Herbologist

To the best of my knowledge, what differentiates marijuana from all other plants is the fact that it is the only medicine that can be used for all illnesses, working in conjunction with endocannabinoids that we make naturally in our own bodies. Once we consume the plant, the amount increases, therefore turning on and energizing our CB1 and CB2 receptors that reside in every single system of our bodies ... endocrine, respiratory, digestive, cardio-vascular, lymphatic, urinary, reproductive, nervous, and musculoskeletal systems.

If you are reading this book and have an ailment that involves any part of your body, consuming cannabinoids from the marijuana plant could be a cost-effective way to treat yourself for any ailment, disease, cancer, or whatever.

I sure would like to see what this would do for a paraplegic. I wonder if this oil will help others to walk again or to see again. I wonder if this will correct eyesight, eliminating the need for eyeglasses. I cannot wait to see the answers to my questions! The thought of sharing a moment like that in the life of another will always be most humbling to me. I am honored to be in a position to look forward and help another see a brighter future. My eyes will weep with tears of joy and happiness in the very near future on a daily basis, and I don't believe I will ever get used to it. I will cherish every moment and hold it in my heart forever.

My childhood dream of helping others and saving the world is finally coming true, and I feel so excited and full of love that I cannot ever stop! I must do this and not let anything stand in the way—not my fear that makes me feel like a frightened child and not the words of any hateful person who is too arrogant and ignorant to find out the truth for him or herself! Not the media or the system. No government will ever stand in the way of this movement for me. I will no longer live in fear! That little girl will be forced to grow up and take a stand and no longer be afraid! I—along with many others—have already lost so much. It is our current government, corporations, and any other organizations that are currently corrupt... Because they will fall! The American people are waking up and educating themselves. They will fully realize and understand that there will no longer be a need for government or corporate influence on anything, and the world will soon follow!

I believe that the reason that we must ingest the full two ounces of the concentrated oil to fight disease and cancer is that those cannabinoids have been almost nonexistent and have been lazy and the receptors sleepy and unable to function correctly from a cannabis deficiency—eventually becoming cannabinoid malnourished. The full two ounces will put the cannabinoids back into your body, awakening and balancing out your body to work how it is supposed to. Taking a much smaller maintenance dose after your body has healed will continue to keep your body young and healthy.

I believe that small doses can be used on anyone who qualifies as a Homo-Sapien. Why wouldn't you keep this oil available to your family for illness and emergencies? I want to be able to teach a complete novice how to use this medication correctly and responsibly—no matter where he or she lives. I want to give you the chance of freedom to be able to heal your own bodies and to teach others to pass the knowledge on. God gave us all the right to live and gave us the plants to do so with. We have all lost touch with the earth in the blindness of industrialism.

You should never let anything take your basic human rights away. Don't just accept the word of the government that this plant is nasty and evil. When you realize that everything is opinion, you will take the time to find out for yourself and realize that you have been severely lied to—only to line the pockets of the elite.